# THE POLITICAL USES OF IDEOLOGY

# The Political Uses of Ideology

**H. M. DRUCKER**
*Lecturer in Politics, University of Edinburgh*

THE LONDON SCHOOL OF ECONOMICS
AND POLITICAL SCIENCE

BOOKS
10 East 53d St., New York 10022
(a division of Harper & Row Publishers, Inc.)

© H. M. Drucker 1974

*First published in the United Kingdom 1974 by*
THE MACMILLAN PRESS LTD

*Published in the U.S.A. 1974 by*
HARPER & ROW PUBLISHERS, INC.
BARNES & NOBLE IMPORT DIVISION

ISBN 06 491780 0

*Printed in Great Britain*

*To My Parents*

# Contents

# Preface

The problem of ideology has intrigued me for some time. I first became interested in it when, as an undergraduate, I read the literature about totalitarianism. Subsequently, I wrote a Ph.D. thesis on 'The Concept of Ideology' under the supervision of Professor Maurice Cranston at the L.S.E. I reworked the whole idea in the summer and autumn of 1971.

*The Political Uses of Ideology* is a critique. Each chapter tries to get to the heart of some important idea and then to go beyond it. As political philosophy must proceed in this way I make no apology for it. Nonetheless the procedure commonly suffers from creating a misleading impression of nihilism. I hope I have not created that impression; if I have I should say that I am indebted to all those I have criticized.

My greatest personal debts in the preparing of this book are to John Bosomworth, Michael Clarke, Maurice Cranston and Fred Rosen, who have read, or, as in Professor Cranston's case, several times reread it and helped me to make it better. Chapters 2 and 3 formed the basis of a paper, 'Marx's Concept of Ideology', which *Philosophy* published in April 1972. The editor has kindly consented to my reusing the material. Peter McIntyre prepared the index.

H. M. D.

*Edinburgh*
*August 1973*

# Introduction

The powerful political ideas of our time are almost all part of some ideology or other. To be sure, outposts of scholarship are to be found here and there in the intellectual landscape. Political philosophy is kept alive in a few lonely outposts, and somewhere there must be someone who can understand concrete political activity in the abstract categories of behavioural political science. But most of us see politics come to grips with the political world, and commit what paltry political acts we do commit under the influence of some ideology or other.

Specific ideologies come and go. This does not affect the issue. Particular ideologies seem to arise to meet some new-felt need and disappear the next day. Like Marxism, they splinter off into a dozen warring factions. Some, Liberalism for example, grow strong as they meet new challenges. Others – one thinks first of Positivism – are stillborn and never achieve much success. Some acquire a different guise in each country; nationalism is the obvious example. Others, sometimes the most sensible and needed of all, like C.N.D., die for no very obvious reason. Yet they are collectively the only serious vessels in which political ideas are transmitted in our age.

For this reason alone, they are an important part of twentieth-century politics; for this reason we need to come to grips with ideology. Surprisingly, in view of their manifest importance, we are largely ignorant about ideologies. We do not know how many people actually believe in ideologies. We do not even know how many people understand the ideologies they purport to believe in. We do not know, in any satisfactory way, what effect belief has on a person or a policy.

A number of authors attribute the singular nastiness of contemporary tyranny to the work of ideology; but little is certain. We have a number of interesting studies of specific ideologies – Lichtheim's *Marxism*, to cite a popular example – but nothing conclusive or even remotely authoritative. We cannot agree about how ideologies came to be, in what ways they differ from religions, sciences or philosophies. We do agree that ideologies are nasty things – not something we could ever take seriously, but important because so many of the mob around us take them very seriously. But we do not agree about why ideologies are nasty and, most fundamentally, we do not agree about what an ideology is. Unless we understand at least why we do not agree, we cannot hope to get at any of these other questions.

This book is about why we do not agree. I argue here that our several notions of ideology are each of them appropriate to our own ideology. That is, we disagree because we see ideology from an ideological point of view. We see it as Conservatives, Liberals or Marxists. There is enough agreement between the various camps to assure us that we are talking about the same thing, but little more than that. I propose to explain how this situation has come about. I also offer some reflections on what this means for our politics. I do not propose to play God; that is, I do not propose my own definition of ideology from some putatively objective point of view above the fray. Aside from not claiming such a point of view, I cannot see the point. Who would listen?

This book is divided into three parts. In the first part I set out the various definitions of ideology which occur in writing directed primarily to intellectual audiences. I argue that the history of the usage of the term is considerably more complex than is usually appreciated. The word was invented by Destutt de Tracy and used to describe a school of thought Destutt de Tracy tried to found. Napoleon attacked de Tracy and Marx picked up the term from there. Why Marx used de Tracy's term is not clear. He certainly did not mean the same by it as de Tracy meant. To add to the confusion, Marx used the word in two quite different ways to describe the political and social ideas characteristic of two quite different periods of bourgeois history. Today sociologists and philosophers use the term in a variety of ways, most of them derived from one or other of Marx's uses but still distinct from Marx.

One way, perhaps the best way, to see what is meant by ideology, to see what ideology is, is to examine some writing which is manifestly ideological. In the second part of the book I examine four works, *Areopagitica, Common Sense, Appeal to Conserva-*

*tives* and *Darkness at Noon,* in order to see what there is about
them which is ideological. We also see here how ideologists use
words to make their case. I have deliberately chosen four works to
represent each of the last four centuries. While no generalization
about such a sweep of history can be made from such a selective
sample, we can at least gain some sense of the changes which have
come over the ideological style.

In the third section I argue that the various notions of ideology
current today fit easily into the scheme of one or other ideology.
The ideologies which produce these notions are Liberalism, Conservatism and Marxism. These are the three ideological voices
which can be clearly heard in our world. By way of showing how
the ideas of ideology fit Liberalism, Conservatism and Marxism, I
give a sketch of these ideologies.

# Part I
# The Scholarly Use of Ideology

# I The *Idéologues*

The word 'ideology' was first used on 23 May 1797 by the French theorist Antoine Louis Claude Destutt de Tracy.[1] This author, a founding member of the *Institut National*, introduced the word as the name of a newly conceived science – the 'science of ideas'. He recognized that although the name was new, the science had a considerable pedigree. 'Ideology', in Destutt de Tracy's sense, might indeed be said to have added only minor refinements to the system already elaborated by Condillac. But the science of ideas belonged to a different moment in French history; and when de Tracy introduced the word 'ideology', he and his fellow practitioners of the new science found themselves in political difficulties. The time, they realized, was critical.

The new science of ideas was intended to be the basis of an entirely new social and political order. The scheme of ideology was grandiose, but the *Idéologues* were not optimistic. De Tracy realized that unless he and his colleagues could propagate their doctrine quickly and gain the allegiance of their countrymen, the opportunity would be lost. The open spirit of the Revolution was unlikely, they believed, to endure. The claims of the new science had to be promoted before the old errors were once more promulgated by the state.

'Ideology' was seen as the modern answer to the unscientific past. De Tracy's proposal reads:

Thus, I would much prefer that the name 'ideology', or science of ideas, should be adopted. It is an appropriate name because it does not hint of anything doubtful or unknown; it does not bring to mind any idea of cause.

Its meaning is very clear to all, if only that of the French word 'idea' is considered, for everyone knows what he means by an 'idea', though few people know what it really is. This is appropriate, for 'ideology' is the literal translation of science of ideas.[2]

B

Somewhat in the manner of Bacon, de Tracy believed that the mistaken philosophic concepts of the past were based on metaphysics; by building the future social order on the certainties of science, the old errors could be avoided. A report of de Tracy's proposal in the *Décade Philosophique* noted this intention :

> Citizen Tracy . . . has given two papers on the analysis of thinking or rather the faculty of perceiving – he suggests that the science which results from this analysis should be called *ideology*, or science of ideas, so as to distinguish it from the old 'metaphysics'. He admits that this science is still very new and can put forward nothing more than truisms. This despite its empirical basis, usually the ground of fruitful research, especially in the exact sciences; and notwithstanding the work of many famous men.[3]

In giving a name to the 'science of ideas', de Tracy hoped to have it recognized by a wider public, but the name was introduced only after the theory of the school was well advanced and a programme of propagation decided upon. In effect, what the *Idéologues* did was to take the anti-metaphysical arguments which had been articulated in the past, whether by the English empiricists or the French *Philosophes*, and use them to attack the established institutions of French society, and as a guide towards creating new 'scientific institutions'.

It is impossible to say with any confidence who the members of the school were. Certainly de Tracy and Cabanis were its leading theorists. With them one often sees listed the Comte de Volney, Joseph Garat, François Daunou and several others who were associated with the school to a greater or lesser extent : Sieyès, for example, and Talleyrand, Benjamin Constant, Andrieux Chénier, Ginguené and J. B. Say.[4] The debt that these *Idéologues* owed to earlier philosophers was in some ways more negative than positive. What they found in common between Bacon, Descartes, Locke and Condillac was an anti-Scholastic posture which they admired. As the *Idéologues* saw it, each of these earlier philosophers was trying to break down the bonds of medieval thought. Thus Descartes was honoured for attacking the Scholastics and for his attempt to build a system from basic principles; but most of Cartesianism, including that central tenet of his theory, the doctrine of innate ideas, was rejected. Baconian empiricism was more to their liking. Garat, paraphrasing Bacon's statement about the idols which beset men's minds, declared that 'Bacon has been the first to break the statues and idols created in the temples of scholasticism'.[5] His sympathies with Locke were even stronger: 'Locke was the originator of the greatest and most useful revolution in philosophy.'[6] Locke led the *Idéologues* to Condillac. The *Essai sur l'Origine des Connaissances Humaines* (1746), a work much admired by the *Idéologues*, was intended to 'determine the extent and boundaries of our knowledge and to renovate the human understanding altogether'.[7]

For Condillac, the Lockian theory of perception was primarily a heuristic principle. He adopted it because it gave a method for discriminating between truth and illusion. By 'analysing' all statements according to empirical criteria, the erroneous ones could be discovered and then eliminated. Perhaps the most important of the ideas which could be dismissed in this manner is that of 'first cause'. Condillac believed that the search for the basis of things, the first cause, was one of the primary factors leading to the mystification of men's thought. The application of Condillac's technique of elimination banishes this quest from philosophy. The *Idéologues* went a stage further: from the banishment of first causes to the destruction of the *ancien régime* there seemed only a little leap; and this was the leap they made. 'Analysis' had not only succeeded metaphysics as the queen of the sciences: they hoped to enthrone it also as the queen of society.

Once language has been purged of the old mistaken concepts, said the *Idéologues*, correct reasoning will prevail. Condillac associates evil with error, and error with the faulty reasoning engendered by linguistic inadequacies.[8] He was hopeful enough to believe that when the source of error has been discovered, the errors themselves can be readily eliminated. This led to the notion that re-education is the key to salvation. All that remains for the preparation of the just society is the establishment of a proper school system. Once the new correct ideas have been disseminated in the place of traditional errors, reason will guide men to the solution of their problems.

Among the *Idéologues* these ideas influenced de Tracy and Cabanis most. The most important departure that de Tracy made from Cabanis's thought concerns the epistemological doctrine: he has a different theory about men's perception of an external world.

For de Tracy the external world is known because of the resistance it offers to our will and action.[9] This small change is the basis of much of the difference in their views.[10]

According to de Tracy, there is no sensory perception which corresponds to either 'soul' or 'mind'; hence these ideas are not meaningful. Deprived of these ideas, and hence of the usual distinction between men and animals, de Tracy concludes that there is indeed no essential difference between them. The most general of the studies devoted by the *Idéologues* to man is seen by them as a part of zoology. This is made clear in de Tracy's definition of ideology: 'We have only an incomplete knowledge of an animal if we know nothing of its intellectual capacity. Ideology is part of zoology and it is in man that this part is important and deserves to be explored.'[11]

Having discovered a method of establishing the good regime, de Tracy could not rest content until this regime was established. As a result of this impatient preoccupation with the social application of the theory, 'ideology' soon came to stand for the theory of government and the programme of political action which the *Idéologues* built upon their science.[12] Cabanis insisted on the propriety of this extension:

> Since Locke, Helvétius and Condillac, metaphysics has been reduced to the knowledge of the process which man must follow in the pursuit of truth, whether this pursuit deals with man, or with knowledge of the non-human world. It can be applied in physical and moral sciences, and in the arts; the principles can be developed and examples adduced, in the laboratory of a chemist, or even in the workshop of the simplest artisan, as in the 2nd form of the Institut or in the schools of logic, grammar and legislation.[13]

The *Idéologues* were moderate republicans. They were all students of, and sympathizers with, the Enlightenment tradition. Again, it was de Tracy among the *Idéologues* who worked out his theory with the greatest consistency. His most important book, in this regard, is the *Treatise on Political Economy*, which first appeared (in English) in the United States because it was only there, through the influence of Thomas Jefferson, that it could find a publisher at all. It must, however, be admitted that there is little in the book pertaining to politics which cannot be found in the works of Adam Smith, a man de Tracy much admired.

The central argument of the book is that man's great complexity, his distinctive feature, manifests itself in social relations, in his ability to make exchanges. It is this ability which effectively distinguishes man from the other animals. There are three possible sorts of social relations, or exchanges: (1) barter of services; (2) barter of things; (3) common operations.[14] Animals, lacking language (i.e. reason), cannot make exchanges and hence have no real property. For exchanging, or commerce, is the whole of society. The use of language in society enables men to operate concurrently. It is this concurrence of human endeavour, along with the increase and preservation of knowledge and the division of labour, which constitute the benefits of society.

De Tracy goes on to expand his theory to include a general statement of the role and function of industry, of capital, of consumers and money.[15] The aim, as he expresses it, is:

> Much less to exhaust all the details of the moral sciences than to see how they are derived from our nature, and from the conditions of our existence, in order to detect with certainty the errors which may have fallen into them by not ascending to this source of all we are and all we know.[16]

Man enters the world, in his view, with nothing but sensibility. Man is sentient but not sensible. Since men can be ranked better or worse only on grounds of sensibleness or reason or intelligence, and since de Tracy thinks men equals on these grounds, he thinks us fundamentally equal to one another. A society could be just only if it treated all men as being fundamentally equal. There was no reconciling the palpable inequality of the *ancien régime* with this logic. Inequality – all too evident in France – could not be supported by reference to de Tracy's concept of human nature. De Tracy could find no reason for inequality and so he sought to eliminate it. Something had gone seriously wrong with French society; the application of analysis could save it. Ideology could be used to vindicate the destruction of the *ancien régime*:

> . . . the greater part of the useful labour of the inhabitants of France was employed each year in producing the riches which formed the immense revenue of the court, and of all the rich classes of society; and those revenues were almost entirely

consumed in the expenditures of luxury: that is to say, in paying an enormous mass of population, who produced nothing but the enjoyment of some men.[17]

After the *rentier* class had been delivered of its luxury:

> In a moment almost the whole of these revenues have passed into the hands of the new government, partly into those of the labouring class. They fed also all those who derived their subsistence from them: but their labour was applied to useful or necessary things; and it had sufficient to defend the state from without and to increase its productions from within.[18]

One of the reasons why de Tracy was concerned to name his science after conceiving it was his belief that a new name would make its originality apparent to the public. Securing popular support was important to him because he wanted a popular government to establish his ideology as the basis of public instruction. By capturing the popular imagination, he believed he could create enough public support for his doctrine to have it adopted by the state. Hence the important part which his science assigns to a theory of propaganda and a political programme.

De Tracy writes:

> . . . if we have well exposed the results of the actions of men, and the effects of their passions, it seems that it will be easy to indicate the rules which they ought to prescribe to themselves. This would be the true spirit of laws and the best conclusion to a treatise on the will.[19]

The propaganda and the programme are contained in de Tracy's last work, the *Elements of Ideology*. Whereas in previous works he had outlined his doctrine, in this last work he attempted to show men how to make these doctrines practicable. He insisted that the doctrine must be generally accepted, even by those whose interests might be opposed to its enactment.

A position which holds that anything is possible, provided only that all (or most) men agree to it, cannot resist turning to rhetoric for its implementation. This is the final turn which de Tracy and the *Idéologues* took.

On this basis, ideology could not remain content to stay aloof from politics. The *Idéologues* had to attempt to influence the state.

It was relatively easy for them to do this as all were members of the French Senate and took part in the drafting of the Constitutions of the years III and VIII; they played a dominant role in establishing an educational system and were all members of the same party in the constitutional and legal struggles. They engaged in all this activity in the name of their new science. But there is an interesting contradiction in their programme which is noticeable from the first. Their doctrines led them to believe that changing popular creeds would change society, but even so the *Idéologues* acted not to change creeds but to change laws. If the paradox of this situation struck them, there is no record to show it.

Their political opportunity came with the Thermidorian reaction. After the Terror they were the only group in the Senate with a plan and a cohesive body of supporters. Ostensibly the Convention, of which they were members, ought to have pronounced an Organic Law and then disbanded, but little objection was raised when the Convention decided to retain control. The Constitution written by the Convention was less egalitarian than might have been expected. The bald truth was that the members of the Convention, the *Idéologues* among them, saw their class as the only one fit to rule. These members of the Convention did more than usurp power for themselves. They passed a number of important laws, two of which, the laws relating to the separation of Church and State, and to education, were almost solely the work of the *Idéologues*. The intention of these laws was simple: it was to deprive the Catholic Church of its influence. They were relatively easy to pass at that moment because the Church had recently discredited itself by supporting the Royalist cause.

The *Idéologues* not only believed that a good state could be brought into being by good education; they went on to suggest that the old evil was due in large measure to the acceptance of evil education. The natural goodness of man could be encouraged by the positively good state; and equally, current corruption was almost wholly the result of the positive state gone wrong. The recurrence of this disaster must be prevented, and the chief means of prevention was the suppression of the educators with mistaken ideas – to wit, the Church. Never again were the young to be exposed to the errors of religious education. The Convention accepted this position and adopted from Lakanal a report which was little more than an apology for ideology:

. . . Bacon, Locke and their disciples by pursuing its method have found in it a new direction, a new light was thrown on sciences which adopted such a method so rich and fertile in discoveries. This analysis, which progresses continuously, but which never goes astray, can convey the same simplicity of language, the same clarity, in all subjects, for in each the formation of ideas is the same: the objects alone differ. Thanks to this method, which alone can do what Locke and Bacon wanted, which alone can recreate human understanding, the statements of moral science, so necessary to peoples who want to govern themselves, will be put under the glare of a light so bright that even our passions cannot throw a shadow on its path. Finally, when promulgated, it will become the universal organ of all human knowledge and the language of all professors. . . .[20]

Under the new laws, private (i.e. anti-republican) schools were to be allowed to remain in existence but the state was to do its best to limit their popularity. Thus the Convention was carrying out one of the main parts of the *Idéologues'* programme.

Ideology had become official policy:

Indeed, education belongs so unambiguously to the first social institutions of a people, the Constitution must do so much for education and education so much for the Constitution, that both are the same spirit, from the same genius: if they are not in some way corrective parts of the same one and unique conception.[21]

As well as establishing a curriculum based on ideology and disestablishing the power of the Church, the Convention adopted other educational proposals favourable to ideology. Among the most important was the establishment, at the head of the school system, of an *Institut*. This body was to be the meeting-place for intellectuals in the various disciplines as well as the administrative head of French schooling. The *Idéologues* dominated the Second Class of the *Institut* and it was here that de Tracy's works were first read.

This application of intellectual construction to society was the most interesting thing done by the *Idéologues*. For despite their success in the Convention the *Idéologues* remained blind to the exigencies of politics. Having established their *Institut* and its attendant school system, they retired from active politics. When the Directory, which supported their schools, was threatened by Napoleon they failed to realize the danger. On the contrary, they supported this enemy of the regime. Then, in the event, they lost influence and all power with the fall of the Directory. And it was during the process of this collapse that the word 'ideology' acquired the opprobrium which it has never wholly escaped. But even without Napoleon's interdiction, it is doubtful that ideology would have been a success. Their schools were threatened with internal difficulties almost from the start.

Aside from the Second Class of the *Institut*, the *Idéologues* were unable to control any of the institutions they had created: the other classes of the *Institut*, for example, quickly reverted to Royalist sentiments. Even the professors in the *École Normale* ignored the important courses on ideology and went back to their pre-revolutionary syllabus. But even if the government had had enough money properly to finance this educational system, it is probable that the inadequacies of the *Idéologues'* theory would have given the system trouble sooner or later. For if it is true that all men's behaviour is governed by their education, the *Idéologues* ought to have expected considerable resistance to the new syllabus from parents.

If, as the *Idéologues* believed, the character of each generation is determined by its schooling, the minds of each generation of parents will be moulded by the teaching of the past. Thus the generation of parents whose children the *Idéologues* wished to teach would prefer the old Catholic education. The *Idéologues* seemed to have ignored this danger. They did not even take the elementary precaution of creating a tutorial monopoly. On the contrary, they tolerated the concurrent existence of Church schools. It was as if they thought that the mere opportunity to go to Ideological schools would be sufficient to attract popular support. Had they been less anxious to dismiss the errors of the past they might have heeded some of its lessons.

Plato, for example, suggested, among other difficulties, that even a perfect education could induce political reform only if everyone over the age of ten were dismissed from the community. Nearer their own time and place, Rousseau, for all his sins, provides an example of greater realism. Rousseau recognized, for reasons similar to those that impressed Plato, that creating a generation of young innocents is no way to change the world. Firstly, it is no way to change the world because their parents (I speak metaphorically: Rousseau's 'student' Émile is an orphan) would not allow the lesson to be taught. Secondly, because even if innocents can be protected from corruption during the period of their education, they would merely be prepared for a rude shock on the day after prize-giving. But the *Idéologues* lacked the sense to take these warnings seriously. The naïveté which was to cost them dear when they supported Napoleon also betrayed them here.

When Napoleon came to power, he was soon to dismiss the *Idéologues* as annoying, tiresome theorists. It is difficult to disagree. If the *Idéologues* were like the lesser Sophists in placing all faith in their power to move men with words, then Napoleon was a Thrasymachus, even a Machiavelli, in his faith in the ability of force of arms to impose those beliefs found to be convenient. And given Napoleon's attitude to religion and his desire for a religious creed strong enough to support his regime, a conflict with the *Idéologues* was bound to occur.

Napoleon's attack on the *Idéologues* was, until the last year of his rule, a temperate private affair among former friends. He had become a member of the *Institut* with their help and continued, almost to the moment of his Russian campaign, to flatter various *Idéologues* personally.[22] But for reasons of state he decided to reinstate the religious education and restore the influence of the Catholic Church, if only because the Church's hold on the people was greater than the *Idéologues'* hold. Compared to entrenched religion, ideology proved impotent.

# 2 Marx's Concept of Ideology as False Consciousness

After the failure of de Tracy's attempts to reform France, ideology was little heard of. The *Idéologues'* attempt at putting the ideas of the Enlightenment into practice might have been covered by the obscurity it almost deserves had it not been for Marx's poignant use of de Tracy's 'ideology'. Between de Tracy and Marx the word 'ideology' is used, without any great attention being paid to it, by a small number of writers. Talleyrand, writing in defence of Roman Catholicism, attacks de Tracy's school. Sir Walter Scott notices Napoleon's brush with the *Idéologues*. John Adams and Thomas Jefferson speak of de Tracy's work in their correspondence. And Jeremy Bentham mentions the new school in his correspondence. None of these references seems to point to any great interest: even Jefferson gave up on the *Idéologues* after showing some interest. Indeed, had Marx not used it, 'ideology' would almost certainly have become an anachronism.

Despite the unanimity of scholarly opinion to the contrary, there is a radical hiatus between de Tracy's and Marx's use of the term. Lichtheim, Plamenatz and Cox assert, on the contrary, that de Tracy and Marx were working with the same concept.[1] Marx is said merely to have refined it. If one is going to maintain, as the scholars want to, that there is some real meaning to 'ideology', then it is important to say something of this sort about Marx's use of the term. Unfortunately it is simply not a tenable position. The connection between Marx and de Tracy may be worth examining as a preliminary to understanding Marx.

Marx read de Tracy's work. We know this from references to de Tracy in Marx's work. The earliest reference is in *The Holy Family* (1845). It shows unequivocally that he knew of Napoleon's attack on the *Idéologues*.[2] The earliest systematic use of the term occurs in *The German Ideology*, which Marx wrote with Engels immediately after *The Holy Family*. Marx also mentions de Tracy several times in passing in his later economic works. We cannot say for sure, but it seems most unlikely that Marx knew of de Tracy or of Napoleon's attachment to the *Idéologues* two years earlier when he wrote his *Critique of Hegel's Philosophy of Right*. Had he done so, he would surely have described Hegel's work as ideological, for it is ideological in precisely the sense that the word is used in *The German Ideology*. Moreover the whole force of the *Critique* is that Hegel's *Philosophy of Right* is ideological.

If Marx was borrowing de Tracy's word and using it in anything like de Tracy's sense, he would certainly have mentioned the fact. Marx was a conspicuously and scrupulously honest scholar. Witness his debt to Smith and Ricardo: Marx never tires of complimenting these predecessors even when he completely disagrees with the force of their work. Yet his every mention of de Tracy is contemptuous. De Tracy is only barely saved from scathing contempt when being compared to an even more foolish hack such as Max Stirner. In *Capital* the treatment of de Tracy is wholly abusive. Thus, the only way we can allow that de Tracy and Marx are using the same concept is to say that Marx saw the idea in de Tracy, took it out of that context, and abused de Tracy for the help. That contention is unworthy.

It is also absurd. De Tracy is propagating his science, his 'ideology'. Marx is largely condemning a characteristic of most social-political thought. The absurdity of the notion that Marx is developing, in some way, an idea of de Tracy's is actually strengthened by the fact that they are both, to an extent, in the same camp. Both wish to complete Bacon's task of uncovering idols. Both are, in rather different ways, children of the Enlightenment. But it is precisely from this Enlightenment perspective that the difference between the two is so patent. De Tracy's 'ideology' is the Enlightened replacement for the idols of the market-place; Marx's 'ideology' is the idol of the market-place.

The difficulty for us rests not so much in explaining how Marx developed de Tracy's notions, but in explaining why Marx used de Tracy's word at all. That they are both, in some indirect sense, about the same thing – the correction of ideas about society – is just not strong enough reason for thinking them the same concept. We might as well say that Iago and Ophelia are similar characters on the grounds that they are usually talking about the same thing (innocence). Why did Marx use de Tracy's word? We cannot be sure, but there are several obvious ways in which the new word fits his need. In the first place, Marx and Engels were struggling with a new concept. They were thinking about the reason why much political thinking goes astray. A new word was called for. Secondly, the etymology of the new word was suitable. Marx, a classical scholar (his doctoral dissertation was about Greek metaphysics), would have seen that 'ideology' is derived from the two Greek words for 'ideas' and 'logic'. Since one of Marx's criticisms of Hegel and his school – the main concern of his criticism at this point in his career – was that they paid more attention to the logic of their ideas than to the practical world, the word had useful etymological connotations. Finally, the word had vaguely pejorative connotations. It suited Marx's purpose to apply these connotations, which he would have observed at work in Napoleon's writing, to the works of the Hegelians.

In any case, Marx's theory of ideology is much more complex than de Tracy's. And it has two related but quite different aspects. When Marx says of a theory that it is ideological, he is commenting on either (a) the 'false consciousness' which has led the author of the theory to speak in this mistaken way, or (b) the way the theory functions – or is supposed by its author to function – to serve the interests of his class. In the first case he is concerned with the reasons why the author was misled – for all pre-Marxian theorists are supposed to be misled; in the second, he is concerned with how the theory influences people to act. Sometimes he means both, and in each case the word 'ideology' has a pejorative connotation. Marx's own theories are said, by contrast, to be scientific. In this chapter I shall discuss the first of these, the theory of false consciousness, as it was developed by Marx and later refined by Mannheim. In the following chapter I shall attempt to explain the difference in the two meanings and discuss the second of them.

Marx's theory of ideology begins with his critique of Feuerbach's *Essence of Christianity*. In this work Feuerbach says that all central dogmas of Christianity are nothing but highly refined myths. Religion, on this reading, is an example of man's worship of himself. God, Feuerbach says, is but a glorified man. Behind each attribute of the Christian God, Feuerbach detects an idealized human characteristic. God's immortality is only a reflection of man's wish for immortality. To understand the stories of religion,

one ought to turn to anthropology and mass psychology.[3] Feuerbach's object, in putting forward this theory, was not to reject
religion altogether but rather to free it of myth. Man finds his own
existence intolerable and so posits the existence of some supersens-
ible God as a salve to conscience. Thus current religious dogmas,
according to Feuerbach, are false illusions which fill a real need to
express genuine human values.

In his *Economic and Philosophical Manuscripts*, Marx applies
Feuerbach's critique of religion to all forms of thought, most
especially to political and economic theory. Marx saw in political
economy what Feuerbach had seen in religion: a system of human
values treated as if they had some independent existence. Marx's
objection to this treatment is that it inverts the true relationship.
The independence of economic and political ideas thus posited
misleads men into thinking that they are independent of their
social context. To Feuerbach, Marx gives the credit for the realization that man is the sole object of ultimate value and that the
distinctly human quality is reason (or consciousness).[4] The first
step, as Marx sees it, in the releasing of human consciousness from
its present torpor is the 'overcoming' of religion:

> Religion is the general theory of this world, its encyclopedic
> compendium, its logic in popular form, its spiritual *point
> d'honneur*, its enthusiasm, its moral sanction, its solemn com-
> plement, its general basis of consolation and justification. It is
> the **fantastic realisation** of the human being inasmuch
> as the **human being** possesses no true reality. The struggle
> against religion is, therefore, indirectly a struggle against
> **that world** whose **spiritual aroma** is religion.[5]

Religion will give way to history, for it is the 'task of history, therefore, once the other world of truth has vanished, to establish the
truth of this world'.[6] Feuerbach's criticism of religion leads the
way to the criticism of politics because 'The criticism of heaven is
transformed into the criticism of earth, the criticism of religion
into the criticism of politics'.[7]

In contemporary society, all that is naturally human is alienated
from man. The alienation of thought, which Marx sees as the production of ideology, is the final step in this process. He says it is
because previous thinkers have alienated their thought that they
have fancied their work as being 'true'. Marx wants to emphasize

that thinking has very important political consequences. He almost seems to imagine that he is the first to see the political relevance of abstract speculation.[8] Actually, this relevance had often been seen in turbulent periods, most notably in seventeenth-century England. Hooker, for example, gives considerable attention to this question in his *Ecclesiastical Polity* (1592); Bacon notes the social mischief done by an unemployed clergy in his *Essays* (1625); and Hobbes lists misapplied philosophy and Popery as the major causes of the civil wars in *Behemoth* (1641) and repeats the point in *Leviathan* (1651).

However, Marx was obsessed at this time by Hegel, and it is in Hegel that he sees the most exaggerated expression of alienation. On Marx's understanding, Hegel held that the world follows the logic of thought when in reality it follows the history of material change. Marx points here to what he considers to be the delusions of absolute idealism, and this argument informs much of his criticism of this school of philosophy and, indeed, of all philosophy. Marx's interest in Hegel stems from his belief that Hegel was the first bourgeois thinker to have been aware of his alienation from his own thought. But Marx's interest does not lead to acceptance of his predecessor, for Hegel subordinated the material to the intellectual in direct opposition to Marx's view of the relation being the other way round.

In the *Theses on Feuerbach*, Marx presents a rough outline of what would, most likely, have been his definite work on ideology. Here he emphasizes the practical nature of thought and denies the importance of unpractical thinking.[9] For Marx, that thought is important which can change the world. All else is trivial. Only in changing the world (i.e. by promoting revolution) can men destroy the society which alienates them from themselves. The preparation of this destruction is, to Marx, the only legitimate task of philosophy.

To Marx, contemporary alienated social thought – ideology – is centred on the state, not on the real basis of society, property. He sees all social thought of the past as mere political thought in that the various entities which made up the state have been analysed while the institution of property is either ignored or taken for granted. This political emphasis is a sign of the extent of alienation; and only when thinking is directed to the real basis of society will it cease to be alienated. Proudhon, according to Marx, was the first theorist to see this truth.[10] The thesis of *The Holy Family*, as well as of *The German Ideology* and the *Theses on Feuerbach*, is that German thinkers have failed to realize the fundamental advance made by materialist philosophy and are still talking of revolutions in thought. Hegel is the source of the error; from him these writers have learned 'the art of changing "real objective" chains that exist "outside me" into "mere ideal", "mere subjective" chains existing "in me", and thus to change all "exterior" palpable struggles into pure struggles of thought'.[11] Against this sort of inversion, so characteristic of ideologies, Marx sets his 'scientific' study of property relations.

One of the tasks undertaken in *The German Ideology* is the provision of a history of the alienation of thought from its prehistoric beginnings to the present distortions. In the beginning, Marx suggests, all men were thinkers.[12] The vocabularies of politics, morality, law and religion were developed by men in their primitive social condition. All ideas, and all words, are the products of society. On this view, if we are to return to these basic, unalienated concepts, we must return to the study of real individuals. 'The basis of the study of men must be man; active, working, breathing, man, and nothing else.'[13] Ideas, like the other human products, are nothing more than mental effusions. They have no power of their own.

The theory of 'false consciousness' is Marx's explanation of the errors of previous thinkers. It also provides him with an explanation of how societies are ruled. The 'false consciousness' of a ruling class, its ideology, guides it according to the direction of its own interest. The ideology of the bourgeoisie, for example, is the programme of bourgeois expansion and power. The exponent in this programme is the political economist, who tells the bourgeois how to expand his capital at the fastest possible rate. On Marx's understanding, this programming is unobjectionable, until the economic and social system which is guided by the bourgeois ideology stops expanding. At this point, the ideological programming and the forms of material production come into conflict. When the forms of material production are no longer able to meet the demands of an expanding population, the social system is bound to be overthrown. But before this occurs, a new ideology, one setting forth a programme favourable to the interests of a different class, will emerge. The fact that John Locke was able to furnish an ideology for the English bourgeoisie is attributed by Marx to Locke's having seen capitalism at work during his residence in Holland, where the Dutch bourgeoisie had displaced the feudal class sooner than had the bourgeoisie of other nations.

This means that, on the whole, that system of ideas which tends to justify and further the aims of the ruling class are the predominant ideas of that age. This comes about because the ruling class can control all the products of property – be they goods or ideas. Despite the strongly determinist flavour of these notions, Marx thought of his own writing as being exempted from the charge of ideology. He wanted to lead the proletariat with a programme in the way he saw people like Locke leading capitalism. The capitalist system, as Marx saw it, was doomed. It had expanded as much as it could and was bound to collapse fairly soon. The job of philosophy, as he saw it, was to create a programme which would show the proletariat how to take advantage of this situation and use it to speed up the revolution. The guide which Marx hoped would lead the proletariat was Socialist science.[14] This turns out to be a proper understanding of history.[15] A proper understanding of the past will give the proletariat a guide for the future. It will show that they are the last class and that all the antagonisms and contradictions which have plagued men up to the present will be attenuated once the proletariat, the final class, has established its rule.

One prerequisite of this science is an 'unmasking of human self-alienation' – the task which Marx's theory of ideology is supposed to accomplish. Given this unmasking, all will be clear: 'It is the task of history, therefore, once the other world of truth has vanished, to establish the truth of this world.'[16] Next, Marx set about producing his 'Socialist science' which is to be found in his later works, mainly *Capital*.

But if science promised a way out of the obscurities of 'false consciousness', Marx was unable to follow the path himself. The exigencies of politics demanded a proletarian programme before Marx had time to develop his science. *The German Ideology* was written in 1846; the *Communist Manifesto* containing the proletarian ideology was written in 1848. But the *Critique of Political Economy* did not appear for another eleven years, and *Capital* (Vol. I) not until 1867. Thus the scientific account of man which was to point the way out of the errors of false consciousness was

not expounded until some time after the Communist programme
had already been promulgated.

For reasons such as this, and perhaps most of all because of his
obvious partisanship, some thinkers have never been able to accept
that Marx's programme is any more free from ideology than those
he attacked. Karl Mannheim is one such thinker. Mannheim was
struck by the force of Marx's theory of false consciousness, but so
far from exempting the *Communist Manifesto* from 'false consciousness' as Marx himself had, Mannheim regarded that
pamphlet as a distinctly biased work.[17] Marx's attitude appears
to Mannheim as the result of inconsistency. Marx created the
theory of false consciousness in order to discredit his opponents,
but then failed to apply the same criteria to his own writing.
Mannheim accepts the theory of false consciousness but tries to
modify it to make it a less partisan instrument. He believes, with
Marx, that all thinking is socially determined. The social milieu
of a thinker is of crucial importance in determining what is
thought about and what is not thought about, how the doctrines
are presented, and what they are intended to do.[18]

Mannheim alters Marx's theory by extrapolating from some of
twentieth-century psychology.[19] Just as the psychologists have
asserted that a man's actions must be understood as an attempt to
justify himself and conpensate for his inadequacies, so Mannheim
claims that a man's actions, and more particularly his thoughts,
function in accordance with the position of his class. The task of
intellectual criticism is henceforth to be to establish the ramifications of this insight and, hopefully, to overcome it. No idea,
according to Mannheim, is strictly congruent with reality, nor is
there any such thing as a disinterested or abstract thought; all
ideas are a more or less pathological expression of social discontent. The Sophists are seen by Mannheim as his predecessors, on
the grounds that they too discouraged the belief in truth and
taught universal scepticism; but it might be suggested that the
Sophists would never have accepted Mannheim's faith in
sociology.

The psychological approach, the 'psychogenetic' approach as
Mannheim has it, has enabled men to make great strides towards
an appreciation of thought. Thus:

. . . for example, when I know what a man was as a child, what severe conflicts he experienced and in which situations they occurred and how he solved them, I will know more of him than if I merely had a few bare details of his external life-history. I will know the context from which novelty is produced in him and in light of which every detail of his experience will have to be interpreted.[20]

With the use of such a method, it is no longer important to listen to what a person says to grasp his meaning. The meaning may be better understood in terms of his childhood conflicts. In a broader context this implies that nothing can be learned from a man's words alone about the meaning of those words; their true meaning lies in the circumstances which determine them. Statements are taken seriously only as a reflection of their source. For example, a man who expresses the desire to see a universal monarchy established is really giving us behaviouristic evidence about his conflicts with his father.

Some forms of thinking help the thinker to adapt to reality and some only hide it from him. Mannheim calls the more incongruous thoughts, the ones which are so incongruous that they prevent the thinker from acting effectively, ideologies. The more effective ones, the ones which enable men to break through the *status quo* and satisfy the needs of the thinker, are called utopias. Mannheim admits that a little insecurity and maladjustment in a class is to be expected, for then the class concerned will express its grievance in the form of what he calls a utopia and so overcome its problems.

Mannheim is concerned lest the present popularity of the concept of false consciousness make utopian responses impossible by unmasking them. When this happens, the group which is shorn of its utopia reacts to the situation, not by a recognition of its true position, but by taking refuge in a more intractable pathological response – an ideology. When a class adopts an ideology it is incapable of expressing its aspirations effectively and it slowly becomes increasingly defensive and reactionary. In effect, a utopia is a progressive prejudice and an ideology is a conservative one. Mannheim's clear and unequivocal preference for utopian thinking reveals his personal bias. Indeed, so set is he in this bias that he completely misses the point of the aristocratic 'ideology'. Since the aristocratic classes are leisured, and generally content with their lot, they have no need to put forward a utopian scheme. Yet Mannheim's psychological model informs him that a satisfied, well-adjusted man does not exist. When he applies this model to social classes, he is unable to accept the satisfaction of the leisured as a fact. Instead, the views which this class has put forward are taken, by the sociologist of knowledge, as a paradigm of ideological pathology on the grounds that they go so far as to deny the reality of change, and even claim to possess eternal truth.[21]

Now Mannheim's failure to appreciate the aristocratic position is interesting in a double way. Firstly, it succinctly reveals Mannheim's own prejudices and thereby discredits his claim of scientific objectivity; secondly, it is significant that the class he dismisses as pathological has produced much of the political philosophy which Mannheim is concerned to discredit. His prejudices neatly merge with his blindness to prevent him from taking such philosophy seriously.

In contemporary society, as Mannheim sees it, all utopian thinking has been discredited and each class is adopting its own ideology. This universal retreat from reality by social classes has its positive aspects in that it opens the way for the classless intelligentsia to come forward and point the way to healthy social action. This intelligentsia, which can be drawn equally from all classes, is supposed to be able, for this reason, to avoid the pathological errors of others.[22] Mannheim must surely be one of the most wildly optimistic of all social thinkers.

When Mannheim turns his attention to those practical tracts which are designed solely for a polemical, partisan purpose, where he is on his own ground, his remarks are shrewd and perceptive. His work on Conservatism, for example, is most interesting. In such less ambitious moments he does much to advance our understanding of ideology. Among the advances which Mannheim claims for his work is the invention of the doctrine of the 'counter-concept'. Mannheim argues that when a class is threatened by a concept, such as Marx's concept of ideology, it will counter the advantages secured by its opponent. Thus the sociology of knowledge reveals the important function of 'opposition' in the formation of an ideology. The ideologist, far from being disturbed by the existence of opponents, takes their presence as a reassuring confirmation of the reality of the evil he is fighting. The most important insight claimed by Mannheim for his new science is the realization of the emptiness of abstract knowledge. Why the credit for this should go to Mannheim rather than to Marx is not clear. Certainly it is a hallmark of the theory of false consciousness as it appears in both their works.

# 3 Marx's Concept of Ideology as Apology

Marx's theory of man and society is sometimes called historical materialism. As the name indicates, Marx was deeply impressed by the importance of history. Every event, every action had to be understood in the context of the age in which it happened. There are no transhistorical truths. An action appropriate to one age would be inappropriate to another. There were no events – or theories – which would be appropriate to more than one age. The labour theory of value, for instance, arose necessarily in the time of capitalism. It could not have arisen before capitalism, because previous economic systems were not (or at any rate, not obviously) dependent on labour. It had to arise in the capitalist era because labour was the basis of value in such a society and the rulers of the society needed to know how to manipulate this source of value.

What is true of theories is true of ideologies. They suit their historical circumstances. Given that he was strongly impressed with historicism – and this is universally admitted – it would have been very strange if Marx had not been impressed by the way the bourgeois ideology changes as the historical circumstances of the class change. In fact, Marx has two different notions of ideology, each appropriate to the character of the bourgeois ideology at different stages of its development. In addition to the concept of ideology as false consciousness, there is the concept of ideology as apology. This point is lost on Marx's many commentators.[1]

Marx gives credit to those bourgeois thinkers who have made scientific advances, particularly to the economists Adam Smith and David Ricardo. These men made contributions to the scientific understanding of the economic basis of society even though their ideas were biased by their social and historical position. Smith and Ricardo were able to make these advances for a number of reasons, the first of which is that they were very intelligent men. Marx makes no attempt to deny the intelligence, even genius, of the individuals who were bourgeois ideologists. On the contrary, he praises them highly. Even a cursory examination of the terms with which Marx introduced his comments about Adam Smith shows the high regard in which he held him: 'Adam Smith, like all economists worth speaking of . . . expressly states . . . very accurately . . . quite correctly takes as his starting point . . . is well aware . . . it is strange that he did not grasp. . . . Thereby he recognized the true origin of surplus value . . . [he] rightly points out.'[2]

But the intelligence of these men would not have been enough, on Marx's reading, to bring about the important advances. The work of the scientists had to occur at the right moment in history. The work of all bourgeois economists, a group in which Marx includes the Physiocrats, as well as Ricardo and Smith (but few others), would have been unavailing without a timely social background. One requirement for the development of a bourgeois social science was a period of 'latent class struggle'. 'Political economy can remain a science only so long as the class struggle is latent or manifests itself only in isolated phenomena.' Thus classical political economy in England 'belongs to the period in which the class struggle was as yet undeveloped'.[3]

There is no question for Marx that, however important the advances made by these thinkers were, their thought was ideological in the sense required in the previous chapter. Smith and Ricardo were not truly conscious of their position. They did not recognize that they were fashioning theories which would be of advantage to the rulers of their society and they did not realize that their theories would require correction by a proletarian economics. Thus Smith and Ricardo are scientists, on Marx's reading, in the double sense that they honestly tried to advance the knowledge of their subject and that they were not concerned to hold back social progress.

But, as Marx sees it, the propitious social conditions which enabled the classical economists to be scientific came to an end. In part, the end of this favourable period was brought about by the very science which produced it; for it was guided by this science that the bourgeois became bold enough to overthrow the *ancien régime*. This revolution, the first that occurred in modern history, was accomplished by the destruction of the feudal aristocratic order. After this was complete, the focus of political conflict shifted and the main struggle arose between the ruling capitalists and the repressed proletariat. When this conflict arises,

> the character of bourgeois political economy undergoes a sharp change. From the time of the conquest of political power by the bourgeoisie in France and England, the class struggle, practically as well as theoretically, took on more and more outspoken and threatening forms. It sounded the death knell of scientific bourgeois economy. . . . In place of disinterested inquiries, there were hired prize-fighters; in place of genuine scientific research, the bad conscience and the evil intent of apologetic.[4]

In the context of this new conflict, the bourgeoisie change their minds about many things, not least the state. Previously the state had been viewed with suspicion. Now it is a useful tool in the war with the proletariat. Now that the bourgeoisie are in power, it is not honest scientific criticism but apologetic that they want from their ideologists. And this is what they get. So sharp was this turning-point in history that authors can be divided easily into two groups: pre-revolutionary falsely conscious, and post-revolutionary apologist.

No better illustration of this change can be found than from the works of Jeremy Bentham. Bentham occupies a curious position within Marx's thought: he is at once the archetypal bourgeois theorist and the worst of bourgeois apologists. When describing the development of bourgeois ideology in the period before the French Revolution, Marx is kinder to Bentham than when he is describing the period after that event.

In *The Holy Family*, Marx mentions Bentham only in passing. By way of relating the history of Materialism which has led to his own thought, he notes that Bentham, along with Locke and Mandeville, were British Materialists. He writes: 'Bentham based his system of correctly understood interest on Helvétius's morality and Owen proceeded from Bentham's system to found English Communism.'[5] Marx also credits Bentham with founding a plan for penal reform and codification of the laws. And while there is nothing in *The Holy Family* to indicate that Marx took any great interest in Bentham's works, he is obviously sympathetic.

*The German Ideology*, which Marx wrote with Engels immediately following *The Holy Family*, presents a more detailed view of Bentham's contribution. Marx wrote that Hegel had seen that the theory of utility – Bentham's theory – was the final result of the Enlightenment.[6] He explains this theory in some detail, showing its progress through Hobbes and Locke and the French Materialists and examining the relation between Materialism and capitalism. Here again, Marx notes that this theory reduces all human relations to the relation of utility. This is to say that in bourgeois theory, as in bourgeois society, love, honour, beauty, etc., are manifest only in so far as they are useful to the person professing them. Putting this the other way round, the relations between people are those in which they exploit one another. All Utilitarianism, in Marx's understanding of it, reaches its zenith in Bentham.

But even at the moment of Bentham's writing, this social order was changing. Ideology was now becoming more than a scientific theory – it was becoming an apology. Thus, as well as leading the bourgeoisie it took on the role of misleading the proletariat. Marx hints at the change in *The German Ideology*:

> The economic content gradually turned the utility theory into a mere apologia for the existing state of affairs, an attempt to prove that under the existing conditions the mutual relations of people are today the most advantageous and generally useful. It has this character in all modern economists.[7]

In *Capital* these hints become more explicit and detailed. *Capital* was written almost two decades after *The German Ideology* and *The Holy Family*. It is tempting to suggest that Marx developed his notion of ideology as an apologetic technique in the later period of his life. But it must be remembered that he wrote of religion in a similar manner in his *Critique of Hegel's Philosophy of Right* as early as 1844. To whatever extent his doctrines may have changed as he matured, the tone changed considerably. And Bentham, once so unobjectionable to Marx, becomes the butt of severe vituperations: 'Had I the courage of my friend Heinrich Heine, I should call Mr Jeremy Bentham a genius in the way of bourgeois stupidity.'[8]

To some of the lesser figures of the period – Bastiat, de Tracy and Malthus – Marx shows no sympathy at all. Of de Tracy he

remarks : 'There you have the bourgeois idiocy in all its beauti-
tude.'[9] De Tracy is called a 'fish-blooded bourgeois doctrinaire'.[10]
J. B. Say is 'insipid'. Bastiat is a 'modern bagman of Free-Trade',
when, that is, he is not being 'truly comical'; generally speaking,
however, Bastiat is a 'dwarf economist'.[11] No justification is
offered for these comments on the vulgar economists, but Marx's
contempt for some of the better-known apologists, particularly
Burke and Malthus, is spelled out clearly enough.

Burke he describes as 'the celebrated sophist and sychophant':

> After this one can judge of the good faith of the 'execrable
> cant-monger' Edmund Burke, when he called the expression
> 'labouring poor' execrable political cant. This sychophant who,
> in the pay of the English oligarchy, played the romantic
> laudator temporis acti against the French Revolution, just as,
> in the pay of the North American colonies, at the beginning of
> the American troubles, he played the liberal against the English
> oligarchy, was an out-and-out vulgar bourgeois.[12]

The key word here is 'vulgar'; Burke is not attacked for what he
says but for the way he says it – for appealing to the ignorance of
the populace. Burke and his kind are not theorists or scientists
interested in advancing the knowledge of their subjects; they are
ideologists who use theories primarily to misdirect their readers.
And this for Marx is indicative of the change which had overcome ideology: the spirit of inquiry had been replaced by 'the evil
intent of apologetic'.[13]

Nowhere does Marx find this evil intent more manifest than in
the works of Thomas Malthus. Malthus had advocated abstinence
from sexual intercourse as a method of limiting population
growth, particularly among the poor. Only by this method,
Malthus thought, could the earth support the growing population
dependent on it. To this Marx replied that Malthus's figures need
not have applied to future production of food because advances in
technology could make the land more productive. But rather than
letting the point go at that, Marx fastens on to Malthus to abuse
him repeatedly. Malthus is referred to throughout Capital and
Theories of Surplus Value. This persistent hostility is not due to
Malthus's error on the subject of production; it is the result of
Marx's belief that Malthus was a deceiver of the working classes.
Marx does not even grant Malthus the status of a genuine thinker.

'Malthus was altogether a plagiarist by profession'; worse, he was a plagiarist in the service of the reactionary aristocracy.[14]

One can gain some insight into just how strongly Marx felt about this, and how differently he treated the two kinds of bourgeois ideology, by a comparison of his attitudes to Malthus and Ricardo. The comparison is useful because, on Marx's understanding, they were both saying the same thing. That is to say, the *content* of their writings is not very different. They both saw the limitation of population as the only way out of the problem of economic scarcity and the consequent impoverishment of the proletariat. Yet where Marx castigates Malthus for his 'plagiarism', he exonerates Ricardo's 'scientific' endeavour. This makes it plain that Marx objects so strongly not to *what* Malthus says, but to *how* he says it and *to whom* he says it. Ricardo is the scholar, while Malthus is the paid advocate who speaks directly to the people in a language they can understand.[15] In this newer period of bourgeois ideology, Marx has to do battle with the 'hired prize-fighters', and the weapons of that battle are less gentle than those he uses against Ricardo and Smith.

When Marx turns from the criticism of Hegelian philosophy and honest English political economy to the castigation of vulgar apology, he will use some of the weapons used by these apologists. He holds out greatest hope that the German working class will heed his revolutionary message because they alone can be depended upon to see the need for a world-wide revolution. The more parochial leanings of the ruling classes in other countries are not fully shared by the German ruling class, and the German working class is not nationalistic. Thus it is originally to them that Marx is to address his message.

Marx chooses his audience for its naïveté. The German workers are, in his happy phrase, 'virgin soil'. It is in them that his philosophy will find its weapons:

Just as philosophy finds its material weapons in the proletariat, so the proletariat finds its intellectual weapons in philosophy. And once the lightning of thought has penetrated deeply into this virgin soil of the people, the Germans will emancipate themselves and become men. . . . The emancipation of Germany will be the emancipation of man. Philosophy is the head of this emancipation and the proletariat is its heart. Philosophy can

only be realised by the abolition of the proletariat and the proletariat can only be abolished by the realisation of philosophy.[16]

But how is this 'realisation of philosophy' to be engendered?

Looking back on Marx's historical position with the aid of
perfect hindsight, it is remarkable how little he had to say about
'the realisation of philosophy'. We can now see an appalling gap
in Marx's general theories where the theory of revolution ought to
be. This gap – which is all but complete in the earlier works – presumably exists because Marx thought the revolution was going to
occur soon. He thought that capitalism was about to be destroyed
through the weight of its own inner contradictions; and that the
process of its destruction was bound to occur. The vast superority
of numbers of the workers will make them invincible. They will
arise and smite down their oppressors. All this is splendid cathartic
stuff. It has all the emotional appeal of the Apocalypse.

But where, one may ask – Lenin certainly had to ask and so has
every serious Marxist since – is the hand of God? How should the
revolution be organized? Will there be small revolutionary cells
beforehand? Will there be a mass democratic movement? Will
the impetus come from the workers? The German workers? All
workers? Will there be a revolutionary class? Will there be a
transitional period after capitalism and before Socialism? A full
theory of revolutions will have to answer these questions. Only
later in his life did Marx address himself to them, and even then
nothing systematic emerges. It is, I think, fair to say that in 1848
Marx had no idea how vexing these questions would be. He would
appear to have been misled by his faith in the inevitability and
proximity of the revolution into ignoring them. Truly, it is left to
Lenin to ask 'What is to be done?'

It is also left to Lenin and Marxists in general to ask what role,
if any, ideology will have in the revolutionary struggle. Patently,
'ideology' in the sense of 'false consciousness' will have no part.
The Communist Party sees itself awakening the proletariat to true
consciousness. But what of 'ideology' as creed or apology? Some
Marxists such as Gramsci and Lukács have not shrunk from referring to a Marxist ideology, nor from consciously contributing
towards it even when they realized that a certain amount of misleading through over-simplification would be necessary. Others
have not been comfortable about this. The task of Marxists in this

respect would certainly have been easier had they noticed that Marx used the word in quite different senses, each sense to fit the character of bourgeois ideology in specific historical circumstances. For surely, the implication of his procedure is that new senses of the term will have to be thought out to fit circumstances as yet unknown.

# 4 Ideology within Sociology and Philosophy

## I

Sociological writing on ideology is cursed by a recurring nightmare. Repeatedly sociologists are faced with their own failure to make their works free of ideology. Clifford Geertz sums up this aspect of sociological writing when he conjugates a new irregular verb in the English language: 'I have a social philosophy; you have opinions; he has an ideology.'[1] What is so nightmarish about this conjugation is that it reports its own failure. Sociology finds the concept of ideology useful almost to the point of its being indispensable, and yet its concepts of ideology are never entirely free of an unprofessional element of condemnation: 'I have a social philosophy, you have a *mere* ideology.'

Where sociology's claim is to give a scientific account of society, and where 'scientific' means above all else non-partisan objectivity, the claim is immediately belied in the case of ideology. Geertz points out: 'Where, if anywhere, ideology leaves off and science begins has been the Sphinx's Riddle of much of modern sociological thought and the ruthless weapon of its enemies.'[2] So it is.

In this chapter I shall sketch briefly how 'ideology' entered sociology; discuss how the concept is used there; notice some of the immense difficulties which bedevil sociological attempts to discover what peoples' ideologies are; and comment on one hopeful area for future investigation. The major weight of this chapter is a criticism of what sociologists have done; but it should be said here that the picture is not all bleak. The job that sociologists are trying to do is difficult; it needs doing, and other academics, most notably historians and philosophers, are abdicating the field to sociology. For these reasons, non-sociologists can hardly complain of a slow rate of progress.

Difference of opinion exists on every term, but I take the general feeling among sociologists to be that an ideology is, at least, 'an action-oriented, more or less coherent set of ideas about society held, more or less firmly and more or less articulately, by some large group of people'. There is a general predisposition to believe that all such groups of people have an ideology. The task of sociology is taken from this to be twofold: to explain, first of all, why groups have ideologies – the answer to which also tells us what ideologies do; and secondly, to determine what the various ideologies are. It is generally agreed, for example, that there is such a thing as Socialism, that it is an ideology and that it is the ideology of the working class. Similarly, intellectuals, farmers and American dentists are said to have ideologies.

## II

The concept of ideology enters sociology through the influence of, and owing to a strong reaction against, Marx. Marx is reckoned to have fastened on to an important subject but to have addressed it in an unacceptable way. The job is to speak of the same thing in a different way. Mannheim and Weber are the important links between Marx and subsequent sociologists.

Ideologies are said to articulate the interests of various groups. Weber, for example, argues for what he calls the 'elective affinity' of ideas to the interests of groups. His most famous discussion of this notion concerns the 'Protestant ethic'. Weber perceived that certain features of Calvinism, most glaringly its encouragement to accumulate worldly goods, suited the interests of Calvinism. Conversely, certain features of Catholicism inhibited the whole-hearted pursuit of wealth. Since capitalism needed men prepared to make hard work the goal of their lives and to accumulate property shamelessly, Calvinism – the 'Protestant ethic' – was the ideology of capitalism. Marxists have conducted a long argument with Weberians on the question of whether the 'interest' creates the ideology, or the ideology the interest. Be that as it may, they agree that the two go together. The effect of this agreement is to make the study of ideology central to the study of economic and social interests.

Weber, however, does not so much talk about ideology as he

talks about some of the same things that Marx called ideology. Mannheim, on the other hand, takes up Marx's term. But he does not seem to have noticed the different uses to which Marx put the term. This oversight is the basis of his difficulties, and to a very large extent it is the basis of the nightmare which recurs to the present.

Mannheim tried to use 'ideology' in a non-partisan way.[3] He wanted to make a double distinction. He wanted to distinguish between two kinds of partisan thinking – ideology and utopia – and between partisan thinking as a whole and scientific thinking. He called reactionary thought 'ideology' and progressive thought 'utopia'. Thus, unlike Marx, he used 'ideology' to refer to an attitude to politics which was said to be present, in various guises, in all politics. Mannheim's position is thus a-historical where Marx's was deeply historical. Marx applied 'ideology' most frequently to one specific historical phenomenon – the post-French Revolution ideas of the bourgeoisie. Mannheim is prepared to use it to name the ideas of any reactionary class. Since classes change position – they acquire and lose power – their ideas could, according to Mannheim's usage, be utopian at one point in time and ideological at another. Because Mannheim's usage lacks historical precision it is, and is plainly intended to be, broader in reference than Marx's. Where Marx brings our attention to the errors and dishonesty of a specific class, Mannheim points to the dishonesty of all partisan thought.

Mannheim's change has been carried further, in the same direction, by his followers. 'Ideology' comes to refer to any more or less comprehensive, coherent set of action-oriented ideas about society. This further change broadens the reference of ideology and is also a step away from a partisan definition. At this point, Communism and Fascism, along with nationalism, Liberalism and anarchism, can all be called ideologies, equally. No invidious comparisons between healthy progressive utopias and psychotic reactionary ideologies, as *per* Mannheim, are made. Mannheim's two distinctions are reduced to one – between ideology and science.

Still, a tone of condemnation is audible. Science is preferred to ideology. The former bears the proudest associations of modernity. It is related to progress, knowledge, objectivity, and its central figures are Bacon, Newton and Einstein. The latter carried some of the heaviest curses in modern rhetoric. It is associated with bigotry, intolerance, fanaticism and propaganda. Defining ideology, Professor Shils says that it makes for 'dogmatic inflexibility and unwillingness to allow new experience to contribute to the growth of truth'.[4] When Professor Plamenatz defines ideology he thinks of figures like Machiavelli and Stalin.[5] When Professor Lasswell and his students studied Fascist war propaganda, they saw themselves as scientists studying ideology.

## III

In one respect the sociological literature on ideology is a manifest failure. It has not freed itself from the taint of partisanship. 'Science' as it is contrasted to ideology is preferred. An obvious value judgement is present. In this respect no improvement over Marx can be allowed. But why is objectivity sought in the first place? Why should sociologists concern themselves overmuch with whether or not their concepts are value-free? The answer would appear to be that they have been following a mistaken philosophical prejudice. They have been accepting Positivist notions about sociology.

Ironically enough, in view of what I shall be saying in Chapter 7, Auguste Comte is the source of this prejudice among sociologists. More recently, Theodore Geiger has pursued a similar line of thought.[6] Positivism has strong champions, too, among social philosophers. Gustav Bergmann and Patrick Corbett, to mention two who have written about ideology, preached the Positivist doctrine.[7]

Positivists make a radical distinction between statements which report facts and those which do not. The former include (on their view) all scientific statements. As such they carry the prestige of science. Their superiority is said to derive from the fact that they can be said definitely to be either true or false. When confronted with a factual statement, we know how to assess its validity. We subject it to the test of empirical verification (or, in the Popperian sophistication, to disconfirmation). Non-factual statements, which these writers characterize as ideological, slip through this net. They are not either true or false. We can argue about ideological statements for ever and to no avail. Therefore, Positivists distrust

—ideological statements. Positivists believe that a subject of study can become a science only when it becomes purely factual; no values are allowed.

For our purposes, we may class together here a variety of theories about what it is that non-factual statements do. They are sometimes said to be statements which report the emotions of the speaker; sometimes they are said to be statements about the world which cannot, for some reason, be verified. In the first case, the position known among philosophers as Emotivism, statements like 'Capitalism forces the alienation of man from his fellows' and 'The State Department is a hotbed of Reds and homosexuals' are ideological. They do not actually report facts about the world; rather they reveal the attitude of the speaker towards his subject. In the latter case, such statements are also ideological because they are not verifiable.

We are warned by Positivists to distrust such statements because they tell us their authors are putting out their ideas under false colours. The grammatical form of these ideological statements is disguised to fool us into treating them with the respect we usually reserve for factual statements. Corbett likens ideology to advertising and that, as we all know, is wicked.

Dorothy Emmet and Charles W. Taylor have conclusively shown, and Alasdair MacIntyre has recently repeated, two arguments which illustrate why Positivism is out of favour. Emmet's argument, in *Rules, Roles and Relations*, is that facts about polity are, typically, normative.[8] When I report the fact that 'Edward Kennedy is a Senator', or that 'Harold Wilson is the Leader of the Parliamentary Labour Party', I report not merely facts but also values. It follows from each of these statements that Kennedy and Wilson have certain moral and political obligations. Thus we can pass from the fact that 'Edward Kennedy is a Senator' to 'Mr Kennedy has a duty to protect the interests of the citizens of Massachusetts' without adding any additional premises. We are not, as David Hume is often taken to have said, slipping in an unacknowledged normative premise between the first and the last. This enthymeme is valid because part of the meaning of 'is a Senator' is that Kennedy has certain duties. This is so because the factual statements mentioned that Kennedy and Wilson have certain roles in their polities. The business of having such a role is inescapably bound up with having certain moral obligations.

Emmet and, following her, MacIntyre put their argument on a philosophical level. They argue from the meaning of 'having a social (political) role'. One can add a political dimension to their remarks which strengthens their position.

In both these roles, American Senator and Leader of the Parliamentary Opposition, the office-holder has the role because a number of people in a position to do so put him there. These electors had a choice – Wilson, or Brown or Callaghan, for example: the person who was able to convince a majority of the relevant electorate that he was the best man for the job. Now what these electors had in mind by this may almost certainly differ from the ostensive requirements of the job. Perhaps Wilson won because some people thought he would create a Socialist Britain. Others may have voted for Wilson in hopes of getting a place on the Front Bench from him, and so on.

Each of these expectations is different from (although not logically exclusive of) being a good Leader of the Opposition. The point is that whatever the reasons behind the decision, and whatever the subsequent reasons for keeping people in these jobs, they all involve some kind of moral or political obligation. Thus the statement that factual political statements are normative is misleading. The obligations which political actors incur may be different from, or additional to, the formal responsibilities of their posts. Thus Emmet and MacIntyre are right to suggest that values can legitimately be derived from political facts – and that consequently the Positivist characterization of such derivation as 'ideological' is mistaken – but not entirely for the reason they state.

Charles Taylor's point is slightly different but to the same effect. He is concerned with political theories rather than with political fact-statements. He points out that they cannot any more than fact-statements be free of values. As he puts it, political theories 'secrete' values. They do so because they all have obvious reference to the satisfaction of human values. We prefer a political system which allows some degree of political freedom to one that does not. Consequently, when a political theory points out that one kind of political system has such an advantage over another, we prefer the former. The supposedly factual theory does not need itself to state the value consequences of its ideas : these are secreted.

Thus we see that the Positivist argument for the superiority of science to ideology is mistaken. Scientific statements or theories about society secrete values just as much as intentionally evaluative theories. Further, attempts such as those of Mannheim and his students to examine ideology in a value-free manner are inherently chimerical. We can examine people's ideologies and draw up systematic lists of what these ideologies are and describe how they operate in society; but our list will lead to our condemnation or praise of the various ideologies. Moreover, so long as we think of ideology as the *more or less* coherent set of *more or less* comprehensive ideas of large groups of people, we shall prefer ourselves to have a social philosophy. Coherence and comprehensiveness are two important features of ideas. We try to make our ideas coherent and comprehensive. Thus we prefer coherent and comprehensive science to more or less coherent and comprehensive ideology.

Further, the very business of being a social scientist prejudices one to a contempt for ideologies and for those whose political thinking is embodied in ideologies. Professional pride in a social scientist or philosopher is a result of persistent endeavour in investigating and understanding society. The effort presumes that the knowledge obtained is not generally available. But people who are left to ideologies make do with ideas that are generally available, hence the relative contempt.

The distinction between ideology and science is, as it were, a class distinction. Since we work hard for our class position, we are not easily going to admit the equivalence of the others.

One particularly flagrant manifestation of this class distinction was the thesis, popular in the late 1950s and throughout the 1960s, that ideology was at an end. The contention of this theory was that Western societies had evolved, or were evolving, in such a way that ideologies would no longer be needed. Their function, providing the various classes with programmes of action, was about to be (was being?) taken over by a scientific social technology.

Daniel Bell and Robert E. Lane applauded this takeover.[9] Well they might. Perfidious politicians and shrill ideologists were being replaced by calm, hard-headed social technicians – by people like Bell and Lane in fact. The evidence for the first part of this thesis – that ideology was declining – was seen in the cooling of revolutionary Marxist fervour, declining turnout at elections, and reduced trade union militancy in the West (mainly in the United States).

Some proponents of the thesis were not troubled by the somewhat special circumstances from which the evidence was derived, and argued that the decline of ideology was both world-wide and inevitable. Bell, whose collection of essays, *The End of Ideology*, is the centre of this literature, never says unequivocally whether he accepts that interpretation, but at least in this book he seems to imply it. More damaging is the fact that no evidence was ever produced or argument adduced for the second part of this thesis – that a world run by social technicians would be well run – and yet only such an argument could really establish the inferiority of ideology to science.[10]

# IV

All this is to say that we would all rather have social philosophies than ideologies. The attempt to deny this is a mistake. But it is no more than a mistake, and it certainly is not so fundamental as to discredit, as Noam Chomsky seems to think, the attempt to understand what people think about themselves and their relation to society and how these beliefs affect that society.

There is a large and constantly growing literature which purports to relate the ideologies of various classes. How is this information elicited? Broadly speaking, in two different ways: by using opinion polls or by taking depth interviews.

Perhaps the most important advantages of opinion polls is that they yield results quickly and in a simple, categorical form. Polls tell us that '47 per cent of the Lilliputians want to ban the sale of the works of Dean Swift, that 30 per cent do not believe in any censorship at all and that the rest are undecided'.

For politicians who trim their policy to meet the daily fluctuations of public opinion, such information is a narcotic. For them what counts is that a majority appear to favour the same course of action that they favour. Acting in concert with such a majority may provide a kind of authority in a political world in which there are few men of principle. But from a less intoxicated point of view, it is not obvious that such polls are a dependable guide.

Beyond this, opinion polls have two overwhelming disadvantages so far as their use in discovering ideology is concerned. The first, and much the most important, is that such polls must, if they are to present their findings in any statistically interesting way, distort the views of the interviewees. Questions must be phrased in such a way as to lead to an answer which fits readily into a few simple categories. The supposition here is that the interviewee understands the question. A further supposition is that the interviewee, the 'man in the street', has thought about the question he is being polled about. Often the interviewee may be more concerned to impress the interviewer that he is a respectable chap – one who thinks about and understands the topics of the day and has a grasp of their deeper meanings – than to answer the question truthfully. It may also be the case that the list of responses offered is so well planned to fit the likely answers that none of them is an intelligent response to the question. All these problems can be hidden by the form of the published result.

There are also a good many reasonable doubts about the genuinely scientific character of the polls. The validity of polling technique depends to an unusual extent upon the honesty of the pollster. If a historian, like Lytton Strachey, fudges his evidence, later historians can catch him out. If a philosopher produces bad arguments any reader will see through them. No such checks exist on pollsters' activities. One report in *New Society* relates that pollsters for a nationally respected company systematically fudged their results during the 1970 British general election.[11] They made up their answers over drinks in a local pub. Is this an isolated instance? Are pollsters really more honest than the rest of us? In addition, the neat categorical figures which are reported require, to put it no higher, a good many acts of personal judgement by the pollster. Pollsters differ on their judgements; well-trained pollsters are few and often not used for political polls. The polling companies reserve them for their more lucrative commercial work.

In addition to these doubts about what polls purport to say, the very fact that polls are continually used to discover the content of ideologies is itself suspicious. If there were such a thing as 'the common man's ideology', it would have long ago been painstakingly catalogued by the use of depth interviews. For if by ideology we mean, as I take all sociological notions to mean, some series of ideas which are held over some period of time (and not just for a week or two – as, for example, people's reactions to certain specific political acts), then we should not need polls to discover them. The advantages of polls, their speed of response for example, are of no real use. Surely, they are used because they force people's ideas into ready-made categories. We ask people questions about free enterprise, law and order, socialized medicine and race prejudice and compound a profile of their ideologies out of the result.

Perhaps depth interviewing offers a better guide. Here the interviewer talks to a small group of people for a long period of time, seeking to find out in their own terms what his interviewees think. This technique avoids many of the pitfalls of polling. Most impressively, such a technique allows the interviewee to say what he thinks – or reveal that he does not think anything at all – about a wide variety of issues. His thoughts are not forced into someone else's categories. Yet even here there are problems, as an examination of Robert E. Lane's extensive work *Political Ideology* will reveal.[12]

Lane's work is subtitled 'Why the American Common Man Believes What He Does'. This information, and more, is available to Lane through interviews with fifteen men in 'Eastport'. Lane asserts that his fifteen were carefully selected. Even so, all his subjects were White, married, fathers and Easterners; apparently Blacks, women, bachelors and Westerners are not 'common'.

Lane takes his fifteen men to represent the nation. Their representativeness is crucial to the claim of the book. As interviews with fifteen men, the book is of little value; but as an insight into what the common man thinks, it is potentially interesting. On the basis of his interviews, Lane seeks

> to discover the latent political ideology of the American urban common man . . . to explain the sources of this ideology in the culture and experiences this common man knows . . . develop some ideas about the origins and maintenance of ideologies generally.[13]

This ambition is furthered by a distinction between the 'forensic' ideologies of the ideologist, and the 'latent' ideologies of the common man. Thus each section begins with a quote from some 'forensic' ideologist (using a respectable Liberal like Max Lerner, or an even more respectable Conservative like de Tocqueville). The thoughts of Lane's fifteen are then used to illustrate the forensic ideal, or sometimes to show how feeble is the common man's grasp of the ideal.

We must be suspicious of Lane's claims from the first. He admits, for one thing, that the words of one of the fifteen were taken less than seriously because he had an uncommon background. He was better educated than Lane considers common. This attitude of Lane's, that if a person has been exposed to some ideas he is not part of the common herd, exposes several assumptions which underwrite his work but which are not obviously true. He believes (a) that there is such a thing as the 'common man'; (b) that 'they' all think alike; and (c) that 'they' are only marginally articulate and hence can be made sense of only as particles of the whole.

But is there an undifferentiated whole, or are the divisions between classes fundamental? The question is a key one in sociological theory. Some thinkers, Lane among them, take the former, the consensus view; others the latter, the conflict view. Notions about how ideologies work, about how they affect the lives of the people who hold them and the societies in which they live, are different for consensus and conflict theorists. This is no more than is to be expected. Consensus theorists talk about how ideologies bind people together and to their governments. Conflict theorists do not think they are bound to their governments and certainly not to one another. It is a curious fact that conflict theories of ideology are nowhere so well developed as consensus theories. The running is made by those who think ideologies hold societies together.

This fact begs for some explanation. I can only suggest that it is a statement about sociology and not about ideology. Conflict theories are all, more or less, closely associated with Marxist ideas. Marxism is not generally accepted as a legitimate kind of sociological theory. This is very largely the point of the struggle to distinguish between ideology and sociology. The former is always defined in such a way as to include Marxism. Therefore, Marxism and, by extension, conflict theories of society are not allowed to be legitimate sociology.

## V

The salient feature of ideologies within concensus theories is that they are 'action-oriented'.[14] The phrase belongs originally to Parsons. This phrase is apt in three ways. Firstly, because it points to the distinction between action and description which is important in this literature. The point is usually that ideologies impel to action. Ideologies are said to be, to use the technical term, 'normative'. They tell us what we ought to do. Parsons does not think that his own work (most of it at any rate) falls into this category. He is more concerned to describe than to change. His works are intended only to help us understand society. The guiding notion is that understanding does not logically impel to action.

In this respect, Parsons's phrase epitomizes the position of those who follow Mannheim. His phrase is apt in a second way in that it does not distinguish between the various action orientations. Reactionary and revolutionary ideas are the same from this point of view. And action orientation is ideological. This way of looking at things presumes that *all* action orientations are morally and politically equivalent.

This is one consequence of an 'extra-ideological' point of view. An ideologist, a Liberal say, would argue for the wickedness of Communism, or Fascism, or nationalism (or all three). He would probably argue that some (other) ideologies are more pernicious than others. Parsons argues for the wickedness (and benefit) of all, of ideology *per se*. They are all said to have a similar role, to play a similar function. Shils also speaks in this manner when he refers to the dogmatism of ideology.[15] He argues that it is the function of ideologies to protect the minds of their adherents from disturbing truths. Hence they must be dogmatic. Each step in the argument is derived from the supposed function of ideology.

Finally, Parsons's phrase is apt for its ambiguities. Both its key terms are ambiguous in crucial respects. What does 'action' preclude? Presumably it precludes and takes its meaning from a contrast with 'theory' or 'contemplation'. We contrast a 'man of action' with an 'armchair theorist'. By using the word in this way the consensus theorist preserves the distinction between the ideologist and the sociologist (or philosopher for that matter). Shils claims that 'ideology' is always 'political ideology', for it is always concerned with authority.[16] Hence the ideologist is always concerned with political action.

But, as even these terms indicate, this distinction cannot be maintained. The social scientist is committed to a definite attitude to political conflict (in this case to seeing it contained with consensus), and to a pattern of behaviour appropriate to this attitude. This last commitment is guaranteed by the same observation that makes ideology a legitimate subject for social study in the first place. Our political behaviour is largely the result of our political attitudes.

Even this last point embodies a form of the action–theory distinction. The problem with that distinction is that 'theorising' is an activity. We need not accept the full weight of the Aristotelian notion (the source of this particular idea) that theorizing, or the life of the theorist, is the most noble because it is the most satisfying kind of activity. It clearly is a kind of activity. Moreover, it is an activity which can take place only in certain specific kinds of polity and which has certain definite political consequences. One does not conduct depth interviews into political ideologies in all countries. All this serves, I think, to show that 'action' is not a sufficiently precise term to denote the orientation of ideologists. Certainly it is not adequate to distinguish their orientation from that of the social scientist.

The term 'orientation' is also ambiguous in useful ways. The attraction of the term is its ambiguity. It covers more than could be covered by 'intention'; and the additional reference is crucial to Parsons's theory. It is crucial because it enables him to place the discussion of ideology within the bounds of that immense catch-all category 'latent function'. This term makes its appearance in R. K. Merton's *Social Theory and Social Structure*. Merton distinguishes between the 'manifest' and 'latent' functions of an action or idea or institution. Ideologies have manifest and latent functions in society: 'Manifest functions are those objective consequences contributing to the adjustment or adaptation of the system which are *intended and recognised* by the participants of the system',[17] and 'Latent functions, correlatively, being those which are neither intended nor recognised'.[18] This distinction is crucial to any systematic functionalist interpretation of ideology.

Functionalism may or may not provide a useful view of society; looked at as an attitude to society it is surely a genuine reincarnation of Dr Pangloss. Dr Pangloss was the teacher in Voltaire's parody *Candide*. Pangloss puts Leibnitz's view of the world. That view is that everything makes for the best in this the best of all possible worlds. On this view there are no tragedies; there is no wickedness. If thousands die of disease, this is seen as a boon: it lowers the number of the poor.

Functionalism is a doctrine based on a metaphor borrowed from mechanics. Every social institution is assumed to have a function in the whole. If it is not manifestly obvious that the people who run an institution see themselves in this way, then their institution must have a 'latent' function. Further, since every institution, say the Fascist movement or the New Left, exists, it must have a function in the system. The latent function of the New Left is that it enables potentially troublesome radical youth to let off steam. Similarly, 'a group of primitives sets out in all honesty to pray for rain and ends up strengthening its social solidarity; a ward politician sets out to remain tough and ends by mediating between unassimilated immigrant groups and an impersonal government bureaucracy'. Each institution or action is seen to be providing some function *for* the system.

The argument is Panglossian in that it fastens on to the function performed *for* the system at all times. The idea that a system might be destroyed from the inside, or that it might run out of steam, is just not entertained. It should, I think, be pointed out that this point of view is not even a particularly good form of Conservatism, though it definitely is conservative. Rulers who accepted the functionalist metaphor would never be moved to protect themselves from threat. The notion of a threat from within simply does not exist. This really is the best of all possible worlds.

The notion of a latent function is invaluable to a consensus theorist's view of ideology for it teaches him that every ideology works for the common good. Within this theoretical framework there can be no appeal to the actual intentions of the ideologist. Their intentions simply do not matter. For this reason the functionalist may label as 'ideology' many theories or movements whose members would reject the characterization. For the functionalist it is sufficient that the theory has an action *orientation*.

Ideologies are generally said, in this school, to have two functions. They serve some interest, usually that of the leader of the movement or the country; and they help the ordinary adherent adjust to his world by assigning him a definite place in it. In both cases, the functions are usually thought of as latent.

The various nationalist ideologies of various African states are often discussed in this vein. The functionalist assumes that the ideology is only really understood by the self-serving politicians who deliberately purvey them among the people. The manifest function of the ideology is to free the nation from the yoke of foreign rule. The ruler and the sociologist see clearly, however, that the real function (latent function) is to destroy tribal affinities and encourage the people to work hard for the sake of the politicians in the capital city. No doubt cynical politicians and interest-group leaders abound, though it seems to me improbable that Africa has a higher proportion of them than the Anglo-Saxon countries, but these functionalist theories are based on a series of dubious assumptions.

There is first of all the assumption that all the members of a class (or nation) perceive of themselves as members of this class. If we are going to speak of people's ideologies serving their interests, we had better first be sure they understand their interest in the way we do.[19] Secondly, there is a problem about the supposed common interest of a class. The interests of automobile workers might not coincide with that of the working class as a whole. The interests of British workers are not obviously identical to those of Japanese workers. In these cases the ideology of the class will not be their ideology. Thirdly, members of a class may not be able to agree on what their common interest is even with the best of wills. American Blacks, to cite an obvious example, do not agree on how best to pursue their common interest. Thus there are contending ideologies and movements each claiming to be *the* Black ideology.

For all these reasons we must speak of the function of an ideology with the greatest of care. Interestingly, it seems to be the case that such talk is most plausible when it is applied to exceptionally large groups of people over long periods of time. When, this seems to indicate, one wants to speak of broad historical phenomena, such as the bourgeois revolution, or the proletarian movement, or colonialism, talk about the ideology of the movement and its function is plausible. Weber uses such a strategy. He speaks of the 'Protestant ethic', and Marx concerns himself with an equally broad sweep. But when one wants to speak of some smaller group with more immediate goals, it is more difficult to point to the 'ideology' of the class or talk convincingly of its function. One is happier with the notion that Frantz Fanon's *Wretched of the Earth* is part of an ideology of the oppressed than about the idea that the A.M.A. speaks the ideology of the American medical profession.

Why is this so? An uncharitable explanation is that talk about the ideology of a group is only plausible, or relatively immune from criticism, when the group concerned (the oppressed) is itself the product of a vivid historical imagination. Less cool is the idea that when dealing with actual human situations where particular decisions must be made, it is almost never the case that one course of action is manifestly right and the others stupid.

Consequently, we ought not to expect ideologists to produce unambiguous solutions and we ought not to expect people unambiguously to support the programmes put to them. Neither should we be so rigid in applying out neatest analogies and metaphors that we forget to take seriously what people think they are doing. These reflections notwithstanding, there is no question that people – call them ideologists – attempt to give voice to the interests of large groups of people; that some of these writings achieve a fair degree of success and that their efforts are a legitimate subject of research.

The question remains, what lines of research are likely to be most fruitful? It is in this respect that I think Geertz's paper is most impressive. He suggests, quite reasonably, that our study of ideology is hindered by our ignorance of how ideologies transform sentiment into significance. He points out that we have a tendency to put a work, say the *Communist Manifesto*, down side by side with a description of the supposed interests of the proletariat in the mid-nineteenth century and to say that the one served the other. How? This is what we need to study.

In the second section of this book I shall try to apply Geertz's notion – that we must apply literary and philosophical concepts about the meanings of symbols to the study of ideology – to four pieces of writing. The writings I have chosen to discuss come one each from the last four centuries; they are all part of the Western intellectual tradition. I hope thus to give some historical focus to the meaning of ideology in our culture.

# Part 2
# The Development of Ideology

# 5 Milton's *Areopagitica*

Whether or not ideologies could have appeared before the current epoch is a moot point; we know only that they began to have great impact at the same time as the collapse of the *ancien régime*. It is only at this point in history, when the medieval view of the world had been thoroughly discredited, when monarchy had become corrupt and impotent, when many of the best minds had forsaken religion, when the technical barriers to popular propagandizing had been overcome, that some men could muster the conviction and the power to revolt and attempt to begin the world anew. Only then did ideologies emerge.

Nevertheless, the novelty of ideology does not prevent us from looking at the period immediately prior to the beginning of ideology in order to seek out precursors. One such precursor, Gnosticism, has been described from the Conservative point of view by Professor Eric Voeglin and his students.[1] According to Voeglin, it was Richard Hooker who first recognized and warned against the political dangers of 'Gnosticism and the Puritan religion. Hooker warns his readers, in his *Of the Laws of Ecclesiastical Polity* (1594), of those pedlars of anti-Christian doctrines who would rearrange societies to fit their doctrines:

> Hereupon they secretly made their doleful complaints everywhere they went, that albeit the world did begin to profess some dislike of what was evil in the kingdom of Darkness, yet fruits worthy of a true repentance were not seen; and that if men endeavour to purge the earth of all manner of evil, to the end there might follow a new world afterward, wherein righteousness only should dwell.[2]

A not dissimilar complaint was made, less than a century later, by Thomas Hobbes. When explaining the causes of the Civil War, Hobbes blames those who misapply the teachings of the ancient philosophers and misguided priests.[3]

In both Hooker and Hobbes we find a recognition that something new has been added to the usual sort of theorizing. In both
cases the novelty is decried for its tendency to disrupt society. Yet
it cannot be said that the radicalism of their opponents was the
thing which especially worried these Conservatives. In Hooker's
case, the Puritans who worried him so were still very much within
the Christian tradition. In Hobbes's case, his enemies had some
claim to be more traditional than he; after all, they had merely
killed a king and started a civil war. That had been done before –
even if not in England. But Hobbes sought to establish a new
political science and a new political practice. Certainly one cannot
pretend to see in Puritanism and among the Commonwealth men
the kind of root-and-branch change-mongering which was characteristic of later ideological writing. On the contrary, what seems
to have worried Hooker and Hobbes was the emergence of the
notion that a radical change of political institutions brought about
by a change in popular feeling about politics, itself engendered by
a programme of propagandizing, could 'purge the world of all
evil'.

An example of the kind of work to which men of this Conservative stripe object is Milton's *Areopagitica*. Milton's work
appeared in 1644. His title calls to mind the *Areopagiticus* of the
Athenian Sophist Isocrates, whose title indicates the intention of
his work, which is to call for a return to the civic morality which
accompanied the regime of the Areopagites. The older virtues and
the wise Areopagites were recalled by Isocrates as something
better than the present laws. Milton's use of the word *Areopagitica*
points to a similar intention.[4] Both these works were issued after
a period of decline in civil virtue which had hurt the author's
country. Milton can have expected that some of the politically
influential men of his time would have been sufficiently learned
in the classics to have recognized his allusion to Isocrates. Some
may even have known that Isocrates was the pre-eminent
Athenian orator, the man who first used oratory for political (as
opposed to juridical) purposes.[5]

Another interesting similarity between the two works is that
both were 'written speeches'. This form of writing combines
several features of the rhetorical art. By writing his words down,
rather than delivering them himself, the author can gain a wider
audience. By using the written speech rather than a more lengthy

form of the written treatise, the author gives himself leave to present only the rhetorical features one expects in a speech, without having to add the longer arguments which even a pamphlet would require. Seven years after the appearance of his *Areopagitica*, Milton explained that he had written it after

> the model of a regular speech . . . that the determination of true and false, of what ought to be published and what suppressed, might not be in the hands of the few who may be charged with the inspection of books, men commonly without learning and of vulgar judgement and by whose licence and pleasure, no one is suffered to publish anything which may be above vulgar apprehension.[6]

True to his 'model of a regular speech', he adopted the conventions of rhetorical presentation. Even at this early moment, Milton makes a rhetorical decision – to use the model of a regular speech – which has political implications. He will use the rhetorical forms which he believes his audience, but not his enemies (those without learning and of vulgar judgement), would understand.

This ploy could not be used today. Formal rhetoric has dropped out of the curriculum so that its canon is unknown alike to educated and uneducated. The 'battle of the books' which raged so heatedly in the early-modern period between those who favoured the classical forms and the modernists has been resolved conclusively in favour of the moderns. The demise of rhetoric is one fruit of this resolution. Given that this is the case – and it certainly goes along with the informal style of ideological writing – it will be necessary here to spell out in some detail the conventions which Milton is following.

In the accepted way, Milton's work begins with an introduction, there is then a partition, next is a narration, this is followed by a proof, and the work is concluded with an epilogue.[7] In the introduction Milton seeks a sympathetic hearing from his audience by saying that he has only England's best interests at heart. His aim is to promote his country's liberty; this note is to be struck repeatedly.[8] After raising his audience's attention with such noble sentiments, he hints at the small thing he desires: 'if one of your published Orders which I should name, were call'd in'[9] – that is to say, he wants England to revoke the recently passed censorship law.

The paragraph which follows the 'statement' is a 'partition'. It serves to show that the thesis under discussion is an important one and it creates a bridge to the 'narration'. For tactical reasons, it is important to minimize the significance of the change asked for – and yet the subject must be important enough to warrant attention. Throughout Milton's eye is directed to political expediency, and the rational justification of the thesis is a secondary matter. Thus Milton meets the rhetorical demands by ignoring the specific issues and writing in praise of books.

A long historical narrative follows the partition. This narration serves several purposes. It gives Milton a place to establish his familiarity with the topic; it also enables him to allege that the evils of censorship have always been a result of Papal maleficence. This narrative further serves to pave the way for Milton's main contention – that censorship stultifies the mind. Taking the historical narration and the proof together, there are four major points within the *Areopagitica*. Milton contends, firstly, that the Papists are to be blamed for inventing censorship; secondly, that censorship weakens character; thirdly, that licensing cannot achieve its goal; and finally, that censorship stultifies the mind.

That the 'Papists must be blamed for censorship' is indeed convenient. At that point in English history, anything associated with the Papacy would be suspect. Milton uses the terms 'Papist', 'Papal' and 'Rome' in the same analytically vague but emotionally precise way. Between them he has a sort of emotional spectrum. Anything which is 'Papal' or 'Rome' is bad and he can count on his audience to condemn them; anything which has to do with 'liberty' – especially if it can be made to seem like 'liberty from Rome' – will be applauded. The words are used because they have strong emotive overtones; he makes no attempt to give them any precise descriptive meaning.

In asserting that censorship weakens the character, Milton prefers to invoke historical examples. The mind, he asserts, is analogous to the body. Each can become good only by passing through a series of trials. Exposing the mind to evil literature, so far from corrupting it, will enable it to grow. The examples which he uses to back up his contention are taken from antiquity and both the Old and New Testaments. In the previous contention he had attacked the Papists. This does not prevent him from invoking, as a final tactic, the Petrine statement 'To the pure all things are true'.

Milton's third contention – that censorship cannot achieve its purpose – calls for careful phrasing. If he were to argue too persuasively that 'censorship cannot accomplish its object', it would be difficult for him to maintain that censorship should not be imposed. He must make a clear distinction between the effects that censorship is intended to have, and the effects it actually has. This distinction is drawn by making the former look ridiculous and the latter harmful. He tries to show the futility of censorship by stating that much more extreme measures than those currently exacted would be required to effect a legal control of manners.

The fourth and final of Milton's contentions – that censorship stultifies the mind – is also the most important. He takes nearly half the work to develop this point. Censorship, he alleges, stultifies the mind by hindering authors: it is an insult to the nation; it is a reflection on the clergy; it is a hindrance both to the maintenance of truths already established and to the search for new truths. Of these four points, all except the third are fairly straightforward appeals to some special interest. The third is more circuitous because Milton had little reason to think that the disparagement of the clergy was a bad thing.

The other three points are argued 'logically'; his point about the clergy is urged by appealing to the emotions of the audience. Milton addressed himself, in the first place, to patriotism. He compared England favourably to Italy where he had 'found and visited the famous Galileo grown old, a prisoner to the Inquisition, for thinking in Astronomy otherwise than the Franciscan and Dominican licensers thought'.[10] Here again, he associates 'England' with 'liberty': 'And though I knew that England then was groaning loudest under the Prelatical yoke, nevertheless, I took it as a pledge of future happiness, that other nations were so persuaded of her liberty.'[11] The alternative to liberty is censorship: 'But I am certain that a state governed by the rules of justice and fortitude, or a Church built and founded upon the rock of faith and true knowledge, cannot be so pusillanimous.'[12] Whatever plausibility this defence of the clergy has, derives from the association of the interests of a 'Church built upon the rock of faith and true knowledge' with a state 'governed by the rules of justice and fortitude'. This feeble argument is the strongest Milton could muster, for he was out of sympathy with the prevailing Presbyterian doctrine to uphold the virtue of the established religion. Milton tries to avoid the difficulty created by his lack of sympathy for the clergy by appealing to 'a true religion'.

The 'proof' is followed by an epilogue. Once again Milton appeals to patriotism and once again he attempts to associate patriotism with his Liberalism. He restates his thesis so that his programme is made to seem the only possible 'patriotic' one: 'You cannot make it now less capable, less knowing, less eagerly pursuing of the truth, unless you first make yourselves, that make us so, less the lovers, less the founders of our true liberty.'[13] The 'love of liberty' is the key to Milton's contention in both a logical and a rhetorical sense. His programme, he tries to show, follows from Liberalism as Liberalism follows from patriotism. Because Milton thinks of Englishmen as lovers of liberty, he knows that speaking its name will appeal to their emotions. He connects liberty with liberty of thought; for of all the liberties, the liberty of thought is sacred to Milton: 'Give me the liberty to know, to utter, and to argue freely according to conscience above all liberties.'

The actual programme put forward in Milton's speech would have limited the liberty of the press to Protestant writings. Milton does not claim the freedom of the press for Catholics or non-believers. This limitation on the freedom of the press is added, at least in part, in order that *Areopagitica* might be politically effective.

To be sure, Milton attempts to argue that such a distinction between tolerable and intolerable writings is not inconsistent with 'true liberty'. He cites the authority of the Greeks to show that two sorts of writing ought to be proscribed (thus neatly contradicting his own earlier contention that censorship was invented by the Papacy), 'those either blasphemous and atheistical, or libellous'.[14] The fate that befell Protagoras, when his books were burnt by the Areopagites, is cited as a warning to atheists. As well as proscribing atheism, Milton is ready to proscribe the writings of Roman Catholics. He argues that this Church is not prepared to tolerate others where they have the power to impose censorship, and in any case, their writings have a divisive effect upon the people. Each of these contentions seems disingenuous. To argue for the liberty of the press in the name of knowledge and human decency and then deny this liberty to some of the most powerful of one's political opponents is not exactly tolerant behaviour. *Areopagitica* is well within the bounds of Marx's second notion, that of ideology as a kind of apology of a partisan interest.

His readiness to make exceptions to the general liberty of the press is a prima facie inconsistency. Such a regime as the one he proposes would have to set up the same sort of censorship against which he protests so vehemently when it is used against his own party. His programme would require a censor to decide what is or is not a Catholic piece of writing. Given these inconsistencies, we have to take Milton's claim in the *Second Defence of the English People* (see above, p. 53), that he wrote the *Areopagitica* in order to deliver the English people from the yoke of censorship, at less than its face value.

But if Milton is a partisan of the Puritan and Independent causes, he was a peculiar sort of partisan. The *Areopagitica* is not a panegyric, nor is it merely an apology; rather it presents a pro- gramme for action. This programme for action, ostensibly the mere change of one law, but actually a call for the creation of a different moral climate, is based, so to speak, on an argument from first principles. It is this kind of argument – or perhaps one should say demand – which struck people like Hooker and Hobbes as so novel and so dangerous.

In the light of this originality, Milton's choice of the *Areopa- giticus* as a model acquires further interest. He might well have chosen Isocrates's *Panegyricus* or Plato's *Socrates' Apology* as a model. These last two works would have been familiar to his audience, who would have recognized them as formidable rhetorical feats addressed to the patriotic sentiments of the Athenians. The *Areopagiticus* alone among these works makes out a case on broad moral grounds for the adoption of a specific policy. That kind of case seems to have dropped out of sight; Milton renews it. His choice of model reveals something of his intention.

But what, we may ask, are the presuppositions of such inten- tions? What, in other words, must the world be like for people like Milton to wish these things? Perhaps the most important pre- supposition of Milton's kind of plan is that the social world can be substantially changed by human endeavour for the better. Putting this the other way round, we see that Milton could not have believed in any notion of social inevitability. Life must be perfectible. This sounds obvious enough, but in fact it was quite a strange notion. It conflicted with those who believed that the current state of things was the result of some kind of Divine or natural inevitable pattern. Further, it conflicted with the general notion that tampering with the order of the polity was just a foolish way of making things worse, a notion which was even more prevalent in Milton's day than in our own.

Restating this presupposition, we see that it implies that concerted human effort can – and ought to – control nature. Man is made the master of nature. It was this aspect which so worried Hooker and Hobbes, as, indeed, it worries contemporary Conservatives like Voeglin, Strauss and their pupils. The Conservative notion, as we shall see, is that such notions are the very essence of modern ideology.

A further presupposition is worth mentioning. The business of writing pamphlets like this designed to improve political and social morality grants a high place to the political power of words. Marxist critics of bourgeois ideology are apt to point to this belief as characteristic of the bourgeois ideology. Marx, in *The German Ideology*, castigates the young Hegelians repeatedly for their belief that their own thoughts were somehow 'the thoughts of the time' and hence of political significance. More recently, Alasdair MacIntyre claims that an excessive belief in the power of words and an excessive preoccupation with protecting the freedom of speech is characteristic of ideologists. An achievement of the Marxist is, as I shall argue in the third section, to specify in some detail in just what way words can affect political action and in what ways they cannot.

Milton's own programme involves two related stages. Firstly, the law regarding the censorship of the press is to be revoked. Secondly, the aristocratic virtue symbolized by the Star-Chamber is to be restored. There is a striking disproportion in the programme. Changing the law on censorship is simple enough. But it is only defensible if the return to aristocratic virtue has already been accomplished, for only then will vulgar writings have ceased to be written. As his audience would have been aware that no such revival of aristocratic virtue was taking place, Milton is in a further difficulty. An easy answer is to suggest that the removal of the censorship law will itself enable respect for former virtues to reassert itself. Such an answer is just the sort of response which so exercised Marx. The immediate action called for is clearly partisan, the virtue honoured is casually assumed to reassert itself in the public mind simply as a result of that immediate action. Experience shows that, however readily partisan action is taken, virtue is something that never appears overnight. The history of England after the publication of Milton's tract is a good example of this; the censorship was abolished but the virtues of a nobler age did not reappear.

But for its ideological elements, *Areopagitica* cannot altogether be classified as a work of ideology. Milton remained too much a part of the classical tradition to be the complete ideologist. His retention of the three sorts of proof – logical, pathetic and ethical – and of the formal five-part sequence, introduction, statement, partition, narration and epilogue, makes his work more formal and less demonic than are most ideologies. Milton's long, complicated, intricately balanced sentences and paragraphs, and his use of rare and foreign words, make *Areopagitica* difficult to read. A first fast reading reveals little of the programme. Milton's use of the classical forms of forensic speech makes it plain that his intention is rhetorical, not theoretical. His use of the classical forms puts the *Areopagitica* into the rhetorical tradition; it is not modern enough to be truly ideological.

Again, Milton's scholarly disdain for the greater number of his compatriots conflicts with the posture of the ideologist who, as Marx points out, stoops to conquer popular support. A work which makes no secret of its contempt for the uneducated, 'those who ought to hold their peace', cannot expect to win their support. The subsequent renown of *Areopagitica* can be misleading; in its own time it was largely ignored. Not one reference to the work can be found in the contemporary literature.[15]

*Areopagitica* was published too early to be a fully developed ideology. By 1776 the situation had changed enough for Thomas Paine's *Common Sense* to warrant our attention as a more mature example of ideological writing.

# 6 Paine's *Common Sense*

*Common Sense* appeared on 10 January 1776. It was Tom Paine's first important work and the first work of any length he had written since arriving in America a year previously. Paine's Radicalism grew in the course of his life and was by no means fully developed at the time of writing *Common Sense*; but the year of journalism in Pennsylvania had taught him how to express his sentiments in a popular style.

His title is aptly chosen. Paine intends, without overt artistry, to present the 'common sense' picture of the present situation. He uses 'common sense' in much the same way that Milton uses 'liberty'. The subject-matter is laid out so that the logical relation of the parts is unmistakable. Paine takes the greatest generality first, 'On the Origin and the Design of Government', and finishes with 'The Present State of America'. He promises to show that the present situation and action appropriate to it can be understood in the light of the highest principles.

When compared with some of Paine's later works, *Common Sense* looks ornate and cumbersome, yet at its publication the work was noted for its plainness.[1] Paine's manner is less personal than Milton's; whereas *Areopagitica* is a 'written speech', *Common Sense* is a pamphlet. Paine rarely uses the first person, referring to himself as 'the author'. The ethical and pathetic proofs which Milton used to persuade his audiences are not employed by Paine; he makes no attempt to persuade the audience that he is a good fellow worthy of attention. Instead, Paine places himself above the reader in such a way as to lend to the work an appearance of impartiality. Indeed, he went so far as to renounce any royalty on the publication of the pamphlet so as to give the appearance some practical reality.

The first part of Paine's first section deals with the origin of government. He argues that governments are called into being in order to fulfil certain ends, and can be justified only when they achieve them. This again is the sort of claim which Conservatives find objectionable. It is interesting, then, to note that in Paine the claim is made much more radical than it was in Milton. Paine makes the creation of virtue – the specific virtues of freedom and security – the aim of government:

> Here then is the origin and rise of government, namely a mode rendered necessary by the inability of moral virtue to rule the world; here too is the design and end of government, viz. Freedom and Security. And however our eyes may be dazzled with show, or our ears deceived by sound; however prejudice may warp our wills, or interest darken our understanding, the simple voice of nature and reason will say 'tis right.[2]

Thus Paine's programme is more openly ambitious than Milton's. In order to make his programme more attractive, Paine associates it with 'nature' and 'reason', while at the same time claiming that those with whom he disagrees are the victims of prejudice.

One of the rhetorical forms used by Milton, the overall classical architectonic (introduction, statement, partition, narration and epilogue), is abandoned by Paine. Paine's rough and barely literate audience could not be expected to appreciate the niceties of such a classical form and might well have found it disconcerting. By discarding such cultivated devices, Paine can gain the ear of an audience which is wary of the artifice of its enemies, and also strengthen the impression that the basic virtue of his case is such that ordinary common sense and natural reason will discern it.[3]

The suggestion that Paine seeks to convey is that the virtues of youth, common sense, nature and reason stand opposed to the dangers of age, artifice, complexity and tradition. Seen from this angle, the British Constitution makes an easy target. That Constitution Paine admits – he has a way of speaking about it as if it were a written document with a definite beginning – was good at first; but it is good no longer. Englishmen, of course, revere their Constitution, and Paine must reckon with the fact that much of his audience is (or was) English. It is necessary not to insult them. He notes that 'The prejudice of Englishmen, in favour of their own government, by Kings, Lords and Commons, arises as much or more from national pride than reason'.[4]

In the second section, Paine considers monarchy and hereditary succession in general. He begins with a generalization likely to flatter the populace: 'Mankind being originally equals in the order of creation the equality could only be destroyed by some subsequent circumstance.'[5] These circumstances include illicit beginnings, degenerate usurpations and other nefarious activities, all of which are found in hereditary monarchies. Paine dwells on this contrast between the natural state which was blissful and the present artifice which is tyrannical. The parallel between this second section and the section of *Areopagitica* in which Milton discusses the origins of censorship is striking. In each case the odious introduction of some new institution is blamed on some mischievous party. In Milton's case the Papists introduced censorship; Paine assigns the blame for tyranny on monarchy. As Milton took some trouble to explain away the pro-censorship ideas of Plato, so Paine has to explain the pro-monarchical sentiments found in the Old Testament.

He says that the Jews lived three thousand years before needing a king, and that when they did get a hereditary one, it was the result of trickery: 'Monarchy is ranked in the scripture as one of the sins of the Jews, for which a curse in reserve is denounced against them.'[6] Paine hopes that this perfidious beginning is sufficient to establish the inherent evil of monarchical government. His fear seems to be that the Bible will be used as an authority against him. For those who remain unconvinced at his contention, he has only ridicule: 'if there are any so weak as to believe it, let them promiscuously worship the Ass and the Lion, and welcome'.[7] The converse of this ridicule – flattery – is adroitly used by Paine to shift the focus of the argument from monarchy. He compares the monarch unfavourably to the average citizen.

In the third section, which comprises half the length of *Common Sense*, Paine speaks of the advantages which would accrue to the American colonists from separation. Like the other two sections, this one starts with a profession of plain speaking and common sense, but unlike the other two it contains few emotively charged words. There are several rhetorical flourishes, such as 'the sun never shone on a cause of greater worth. Now is the seedtime of continental union, faith, and honour.'[8] But such passages are rare; indeed, the tenor of the writing changes here, and becomes more discursive than elsewhere. Two points are made in this section: the first, that separation is in the colonists' interest; the second, that a democracy must be established after independence.

Paine claims that England rules America for commercial reasons only; she protects America against other powers only because she is afraid of losing trade. He suggests that other nations would treat America as a friend if the tie with England were broken. Paine tells the colonists that they have no quarrel with the Continental European powers, nor would they wish to fight in English wars. The American advantage lies in peaceable trade with all. In the midst of his appeal to commercial self-interest, a matter which Paine can have expected all to understand and appreciate, he repeats his central contention: 'Everything that is right or reasonable pleads for separation. The blood of the slain, the weeping voice of nature cries " 'TIS TIME TO PART".'[9] Paine even invokes the name of God to his side. Did God not separate the two countries, he asks the colonists, with a grand ocean, to make separation easier? Indeed, the path ahead is so clear that Paine is sure that those who cannot see it must be corrupt in some way.

But if rebellion is inevitable and desirable, subsequent events are clouded. Paine finds the lack of planning alarming and proceeds to offer suggestions to meet the need. His proposals, forming a coherent programme, amount to a call for a representative democracy with numerous popular controls of the representative. This democratic part of *Common Sense* is distinguished from the other nationalistic parts in being unemotionally presented. None of the rhetoric used in the previous sections to demand the separation from England is used to put across this plea for democracy. Paine merely asserts that the programme is so perfect that only some demonic spirit could disturb it. The plan is presented in great detail; even the forms of religious celebration are prescribed. But no use is made of emotive abstractions, there are few appeals to action, little is made of the 'inevitability' of the plan, and no attempt is made to justify it.

The concluding section of *Common Sense* is comprised of a long list of the various strategic and tactical advantages which the colonists have at their command. We have not many men, Paine admits, but no matter, in unity there is strength. We have not many ships either, but no matter, we have many harbours in which to tie up England's fleet. The colonists are strong because they have no debt, although they might well acquire one (and thus assure future unity) because then they could buy a fleet; and Paine is confident that the ships could be sold after the war at a profit. The colonists are reassured that the large English fleet is dispersed all over the globe, and most of it is supposed to be in bad repair anyhow. Paine shows, in presenting this part of his case, that he knows how to turn any fact to his favour. These are debaters' points. He tells the colonists that they have abundant natural resources and can build anything they need for themselves, without having to depend on others. If they revolt now, Paine adds, they will have enormous empty lands to profit by; later they may be crowded. Finally, Paine assures the Americans that the colonists are in their 'seedtime'.

However, the first and second editions of *Common Sense*, which were written before the Declaration of Independence, advance no statistics to justify these remarks.[10] In the third and all subsequent editions, written after independence had been declared, many tables of facts and figures supporting these contentions are added. Admittedly, by the time the third edition was published, an exhortation to rebellion was no longer necessary; but a new fleet was the pressing need and Paine's figures make the proposal for such a fleet seem more attractive. Paine's *Common Sense* is a practical work which he adapts to meet changed circumstances.

Paine concludes *Common Sense* with a repetition of the points of his programme, each being made to turn on emotionally charged words, and the pamphlet ends with a hint that a further manifesto presenting the reasons for rebellion should be published. This proposal foreshadows the Declaration of Independence; not only the general ideas but much of the detail as well is taken up in the Declaration.

If an ideology is going to be effective, its prescriptions must be convincing. It must convince otherwise disinterested people that its programme is worth supporting. Paine makes the broadest possible appeal for support. He asserts that the cause of American independence is the 'cause of all mankind'. This claim, as well as asking for support from everyone, has the important advantage of sounding highly moral. Surely the cause of all mankind cannot be wrong. It follows from this that any other cause which conflicts in any important way must be in the interests of some wickedly narrow group of men. It is very much this sort of claim, with its assumption of infallibility and its intolerance towards others' ideas, which worries Liberal writers on ideology. And surely the Liberals are right to point to this facet in contemporary writing. They may over-generalize about its frequency, but when writers like Hannah Arendt and John Plamenatz point to this feature of Stalinism, they are quite right. The advantages of this gambit are unmistakable.

These Liberals, of course, argue that such claims are not true. Plamenatz, for instance, is concerned to show at length that Marxism is not necessarily in the interests of the working class, let alone of all men. Certainly in Paine's case the claim of universal advantage is not true. His claim is based on his prediction that a new republic in America would be an example to others throughout the world, since the colonists could serve as a model for others who could then throw off the yoke of their monarchs. For tactical reasons, this point is not urged too loudly, since the colonists badly needed the support of Continental monarchs, particularly the King of France. Neither is the claim very convincing, for, as Paine points out, there already exist two happy republics in the world, the Netherlands and Switzerland, and their example has not spread. The claim, such as it is, is also circular. A republic in one country will be an example to others only if republics are universally thought to be good things. If republics are universally admired, then Paine's claim that his cause is in the interests of all mankind is no more than a grand restatement of the fact that republics are admired. However, if the claim to universal benefit is a sham, it does not necessarily prevent the ideology from working in the interests of the American colonists themselves.

It is interesting to note how attractive such a claim to universal advantage can be. If believed, it can absolve the consciences of the partisans from any qualm which violent political action may entail. Moreover, it is unanswerable. Who would presume to dispute the virtue of an action which will benefit all men? No one would listen. The effect of invoking such an argument is to place the onus of partisanship on to those who disagree. An opponent would first have to deny this abstract argument; such a refutation would be more difficult than the original assertion.

The notion of universal benefit from a change of policy is

interesting, too, for what it tells us about the proposer's conception
of the decision and for the presuppositions of its being a credible
claim. Most day-to-day political decisions are basically resource-
allocation decisions. Should more be spent on schools *or* houses
*or* arms? Should more be spent by the public *or* the private sphere
of the economy? The notion is that the money to be spent is
limited, so that if some get it others are denied it. These considerations divide people. If more is spent on schools and less on
arms, children benefit and soldiers suffer. Of course, the starvation
of any essential or generally useful service will eventually hurt all.
But this does not overcome the fact that decisions about resource
allocations – not necessarily but usually money – always help some
to the detriment of others.

We say of decisions to starve one or another necessary or useful
service that they are 'short-sighted', not that they are partisan,
because we understand that such decisions are partisan. It is not
usually terribly difficult to discern who will gain or lose immediately from any particular choice, and we line up accordingly to
lend support to our side.

It is certainly not the case, however, that there is no such thing
as the general interest; neither is it the case that all decisions are
resource-allocation decisions. Attempts to argue the latter, or,
more subtly, that all political decisions can be reduced to allocation decisions, are legion. The impressive rigour which writers like
Brian Barry discern in such an approach is bought at the expense
of distortion.

The most usual argument for the notion that all political decisions are reducible to resource-allocation decisions – politics is
the authoritative allocation of values, as Easton succinctly puts it
– cites as evidence the fact that some people are in favour and
others opposed to any specific proposal. The politician is said
to be distributing resources to one or other party. But this
argument rests on a confusion between the subject of a decision
and the factions urging each possible outcome. There is no
logical absurdity in the common Liberal practice of urging policy
not in the direct interest of Liberals. Thus there is no argument
from a party's support for a policy to that policy being in its
interest.

An example of a political decision which cannot be reduced to
a resource-allocation decision – despite the fact that some will

undoubtedly gain and others lose and some are in favour and others opposed – is the British decision to join the European Economic Community. Some opponents to entry try to make the decision look like a resource-allocation decision. They argue that joining will cost Britain more than she will gain and that there- fore she ought not to go in. Aside from the fact that reliable figures on the financial cost and benefits are singularly difficult to obtain – if, for that matter, they are available at all – such arguments are simply beside the point. The point is quite simply that Britain is part of Europe and ought to take part in the col- lective decisions which affect that society. And that is not a matter of resource allocation.

When a decision is of this kind, it is possible that it be of immediate universal benefit. Where resources are allocated, some- one loses; he doesn't get any. This need not be the case where they are not being allocated. Of course, it is always open for a party to claim that everyone benefits if it benefits. Industrialists are not backward in arguing that greater profits for them ought to be encouraged by government action, because this will encourage them to invest and that additional investment will provide more jobs. Trade unionists, on the other side, urge that the wages of their members ought to be raised by government action because that would in itself enhance the general prosperity. But even if one or other or both of these claims is true, there is no serious question that the general gain is a side-effect of a resource allocation and that it is the immediate benefit which motivates the two parties. I do not proclaim the avariciousness of these parties; increasing the wealth of their members is, after all, what they are paid to do.

Thus when a Milton or a Paine argues that his proposal is of universal benefit, this could only be the case – and could pre- sumably only be believed to be the case – if he is not talking about distributing resources. Plainly, neither Milton nor Paine is. Con- firmation that ideologies are concerned with such decisions comes from Marx. Marx is careful to argue that the overthrow of capitalism will occur only at the moment when nearly all men have been forced into the proletariat. This is believed to be one of the inevitable effects of capitalist production: more get poorer and a small number get wealthier. In other words, Socialism – which is clearly a doctrine about the distribution of resources within a special kind of society – will come about only when the question 'capitalism or Socialism?' is no longer a resource-allocation problem. This is not to deny that people are Socialists or capitalists as suits their interest; merely that the credibility of a claim of universal benefit is contingent upon this support being misconceived.

By asserting the universal benefit of his own cause and the evil of his opponent, Paine opens the way for a sort of 'cops and robbers' politics. Politics is made to seem a conflict where one side is right. His cause, the repository of virtue, is opposed to the repository of evil – and what is more, is the only possible response to this evil. The 'cops' can catch and disarm the 'robbers'. The common sense of the situation is the only answer to the 'royal brute'. If Paine's view is widely accepted, it will have the effect of bifurcating the public. There is no room for a prudent middle ground between good and evil. This is one of the chief objections which Liberals, who habitually see themselves as occupying the middle ground, make to such schemes.

Liberals, like Raymond Aron in his *Opium of the Intellectuals*, complain that this frequently used tactic introduces a spurious clarity into the political situation, as, no doubt, it often does. Everyone who does not join the vigilantes is said to be helping the robbers.[11] As John Foster Dulles used to say, if you are not for us, you are with them. In order to play this 'cops and robbers' politics, one has to have a readily identifiable robber. This may seem harmless enough, but as Aron and, before him, Mannheim have suggested, if ideologies do not find ready-made robbers, they can always create one.[12]

Whether anyone else can be persuaded to take the actors in this play seriously is, of course, a rather different question. There is at least some interesting evidence to the contrary. It appears to be the case that the 'McCarthyite' and 'Communist' camps took themselves and each other much more seriously than the general public took either. Most people, at least on the evidence of one survey, took traditional bread-and-butter issues to be much more important even during the height of the fuss.[13] The evidence may not be convincing even about this one case, and it is well to remember that it is only about one case and may not be generally true; certainly Paine did not have opinion surveys to worry about.

Paine's adherents, those who agree with his association of all things simple, young and natural with his Liberal nationalism, may well have felt disappointed by the curious metamorphosis in the third section. The complicated programme put forward there is quite out of keeping with the rest of the pamphlet. This third section resembles a treatise more than a pamphlet. The plea for democracy is not supported by any rhetorical aids. This change of style on Paine's part is reflected in the reception of *Common Sense*. The nationalist sections were adopted by the colonists, the democratic section was ignored.

Paine's change of style can be explained by the realization that the nationalist portions of his pamphlet put forward ideas with which a great many colonists already sympathized, whereas the democratic part of the programme was not in accord with the prevailing sentiments.[14] Paine was unable to redirect the moral feelings which already existed on the question of rebellion to the subject of democracy. He was unable to create new sentiments. As an ideologist, Paine was most successful when he followed his own advice: 'The mind of a living public is quickly alarmed and easily tormented. It not only suffers by the stroke, but it is frequently fretted by the cure, and ought, therefore, to be tenderly dealt with. It feels first and reasons afterwards.'[15]

Paine's partial success suggests that his original boldness was uncalled for. He actually cannot change society with his ideology to any greater degree than the prevailing moral sentiments provide scope for attracting people to his programme.

The rhetorical devices which Paine used deliberately to move people to accept his ideas are, very largely, the creation of the age in which he lived. Classical rhetoricians, Aristotle most notably, laid little stress on these devices.[16] The ending of the clerical monopoly on literacy, the development of cheap methods of printing, the discrediting of the Christian world-view, all contributed to changing the position. And, not surprisingly, Paine and his contemporaries began to comment on the new rhetorical forms which became useful. Edmund Burke's popular *Philosophical Inquiry into our Ideas of the Sublime and the Beautiful* contains what appears to be the first – and what still is in many ways the best – discussion of the subject.[17]

The peculiarity of the new rhetoric which Burke notes rests largely in the repeated use of abstract political terms. The advantages of such abstractions, as Burke points out, is that they commit us to one of only two judgements, 'boo' or 'hurrah', but can serve a great many possible descriptive uses. Words – Burke calls them 'sounds' appropriately enough – like 'virtue', 'liberty' and 'honour' combine an indefinite reference with a definite feeling. None of us, he claims, knows upon hearing these 'sounds' what they mean; we only know that they are 'hurrah' words.

Burke makes the interesting observation about this situation that clarity is inversely related to strength.[18] Here he related an obvious psychological fact about language. His point is that the more strongly we feel that something is good or evil, the less likely we are to have a precise notion in mind. And the words that are able to engender the strongest feelings are those with the least clear denotation. In our time, these notions about the political use of abstract vocabulary have been investigated by Harold Lasswell and his students and Arne Naess. Both of them propose a systematic 'content analysis' of political utterance, the point of such analysis being to reveal the virtues latent in any particular writing. The method of 'content analysis' was to add up the various uses of a word such as 'democracy', and then to notice the context in which it was used. The methodological problems which Lasswell and his students encountered were so overwhelming that they have abandoned the project, which is unfortunate because the systematic use of such techniques could tell us a good deal about the political writings of our time.[19]

Clearly Paine uses his 'common sense', 'nature' and 'reason' in the manner indicated by Burke. Paine is not using them from any concern with a 'precise notion', for he realizes that no such notion exists. Rather he is using them because they endow his programme with stature otherwise unattainable. His single year of journalism in Pennsylvania must have been sufficient to teach Paine the locally popular vocabulary. It is to be noted that where he uses such emotive language he is successful in focusing action, and where he neglects it he is unsuccessful.

The success or failure of a specific ideological work is never easy to determine. It may well be that events in the American colonies would have turned out exactly as they did had Paine never lived. One cannot say for sure; yet *Common Sense* sold half a million copies within its own time, and Paine was strongly encouraged by many of the leading colonists. This does seem to indicate that Paine agreed with and, at least to some extent, focused the sentiments of the colonists. Many of these sentiments turned up again in the Declaration of Independence which Paine had explicitly urged on the colonists. Nothing like this success came to Auguste Comte.

# 7 Comte's *Appeal to Conservatives*

On any definition of ideology, *Appeal to Conservatives* fits. Comte's aim is to present a system for the improvement of the human condition in such a way as to make the promulgation of the system so attractive as to make it tantamount to achievement of the ideal.[1] Comte believed that the best of philosophers were those who changed the ideas of their contemporaries. Comte aspired to this height in order to change his world.[2] He attributes to mere words a power beyond that which most will allow as prudent. He is very like the idealists whom Marx castigated at very nearly the same moment who believed that the logic of ideas – their ideas of course – could change the course of history.

In some ways Comte's position is rather close to Marx's for all the dissimilarity in their respective works. Each of them was deeply impressed by the ideologies of the French Revolution and their near success. Each looked for the thing that these ideologies had missed. Each, too, looked for an unshakeable scientific basis for their theory, one which would exhibit the laws of history and show its discoverer the way ahead. Where Marx turned to history for his science, Comte turned to sociology and sought to be its Bacon.[3]

This conception of a scientifically based programme of political action is fundamental to Comte's thought. The frequency with which mid-nineteenth-century – and later – writers made this turning to 'scientism' has been noted by the Conservative anti-ideological school. Some, like Niemeyer and Leo Strauss, find the essence of ideology in this turning away from the eternal verities. Others, like Oakeshott, while not proposing a methodical replacement for science, claim that ideology is at heart an attempt to impose any set of categories not derived from political experience on to political action. Comte disagrees: any political statement which is not based on science is, he proclaims, a usurpation.

Comte's science, his 'sociology', was to provide the key to action he desired. He saw political history as a sort of battleground for principles; sociology was to furnish the ultimate weapon to dominate that field for ever. It was a battle in which Comte assigned himself a major role. He was to be the Aristotle and the St Paul of the new sociology, at once its originator and its high priest.

History he divides into three phases, the theological, the metaphysical and the positivistic, each of the three based on an essential principle: in turn, theology, metaphysics and Positivism. Each had a champion in the contemporary world. The theological principle was represented by the reactionaries, the metaphysical by the revolutionaries, and Comte claimed himself to represent the Positivist principle.

He favoured a reconciliation of the three camps, but said it could be accomplished only by a recognition of the superiority of Positivism, a superiority which stemmed from Positivism's synthesis of the best of the other principles. From theology, Positivism took the realization that the will must dominate the intellect; and from metaphysics it took the doctrine of the necessity for a rigorous consistent search for truth and a recognition of the importance of a political system based on the truth thus revealed. Thus the exponents of theology and metaphysics ought to see that their own theories had only been improved upon and willingly enter the Positivist camp, or so Comte hoped.

We may doubt that this is a legitimate synthesis. Firstly, it is a matter of controversy among theologians as to the proper relationship between the will and the intellect, so that Comte's recognition of this truth at the heart of theology involves a certain amount of judicious reading of theology. Secondly, it is not clear how this theological principle is to be synthesized with the metaphysical principle of search for a rigorous consistent truth. As will be seen later, Comte seems to take the first principle to mean he can suppress any inconvenient truths when politics seems to demand it and ignore political realities in the name of truth whenever that is convenient to the consistency of his work. This is hardly a synthesis – more an obfuscation.

Comte's most systematic works are the *Cours de Philosophie Positive* (1830–42) and the *Système de Politique Positive* (1851–4), in which the main tenets of his doctrines may be found.

The *Cours* sets out Comte's theory of history and his ideas about the various stages of human development. It dates from the period of his career when he thought of himself as the Aristotle of Positivism. The *Système* is a much more 'theological' (in his sense of the word) work. It proclaims love to be the motivating principle of history and sets out Comte's Positivist ideology. The book dates from his 'second career', in which Comte saw himself as a new St Paul. Since Comte's model for his religion is Catholicism, it is interesting to note the absence of a new Christ between his new Aristotle and his new St Paul.

Although the *Système* did not actually set out the doctrines of the new religion, as Comte called it, it established the general theory upon which these doctrines were to be based. Comte, who was nothing if not widely read, saw St Paul's Epistles in a similar light.[4] But for Comte's explicitly religious writings it is necessary to turn to his later, lesser-known works. The work considered here in detail, the *Appeal to Conservatives* (1855), belongs to this last period.

There has been considerable discussion regarding the status of the later works, and in the light of Comte's mental instability, his melancholy and his suicide attempt this is hardly surprising.[5] Some of those, John Stuart Mill most outstandingly, who were impressed with Comte's earlier works, were repelled by the later ones.[6] Indeed, Mill denied that the later ideological works had any necessary connection with the earlier 'scientific' ones. Mill's insistence on separating the two careers is easy enough to understand. Unless he could disassociate the ideology from the science, his own praise of the Comtean science might implicate him in the Comtean ideology. But letters which have come to light since Comte's death have substantiated his claim that his second career was anticipated during the first one.[7] The matter was of some importance for Comte, for he wanted to be able to say that the ideology was based on the science, and was not an independent or arbitrary construct.

The *Appeal to Conservatives* is shaped in treatise form. This gives at first the impression that the work is scholarly rather than polemical. The *Appeal* has six sections: a long preface, an equally long introduction, three 'parts' and a conclusion. The length of the work, as much as anything, sets it off from Milton's speech and Paine's pamphlet, and yet Comte calls attention to the fact that, like Milton's and Paine's work, it is at least partly a *pièce d'occasion*. It was written in twenty-eight days.

Comte says that his object 'has been to bring the universal doctrine home to those who cannot give the proper study to its systematic explosion.'[8] In other words, it is a popularization of his earlier work. In the pamphlet he is trying to show that the Conservative school of thought is now ripe to lead a new cause. He is also, as it were, picking the fruit. The Conservative inclination to 'conserve while improving' must be mated, Comte insists, to the Positivist doctrine. Such a union

> is the aim of this pamphlet, which represents the final transition as destined to mark the third generation of the exceptional century, the two first generations of which were, the one originally retrograde and revolutionary. The two considerations, religious and political, of this inauguration have been separately fulfilled; it remains only to combine them through an adequate accord between the universal synthesis and the paramount will.[9]

Comte lived in a neat world. In one sense it must be admitted that Comte's work is a synthesis of religion and science. His inflated, abstract, earnest rhetoric, which so badly calls for deflating, calls to mind at once the infuriating pomposity of religious twaddle and scientific cant. But this is surely not the level on which Comte thought he was synthesizing the two, even though it may account for some of his popularity. His aim, he proclaims in the preface, is to make possible both order and progress; pompous though he is, he is expressing something which a good number of his contemporaries in France and Britain found attractive.

One thing Comte was determined against was disorder, messiness and chance. He wanted things to be neatly planned and yet not repressive. I know of no studies which describe the membership of the various national Positivist societies. In lieu of such work, it is perhaps permissible to speculate that the *Appeal to Conservatives* went exactly to Conservatives; to those who were frightened by the Revolution and yet willing to recognize that what had been done could not be undone. That the vicissitudes of the present were to be attributed to the revolutionary philosophies he had no doubt. The revolutionary philosophy had been, he thought, inadequate; they could not sustain a regime for long because they had not understood human psychology.

Positivism requires a radical change first in human nature and then in society. Change in man as in society is possible, Comte tells us, because exercise can develop latent tendencies while other tendencies will atrophy in time through disuse. The aggressive tendencies, which Comte associated with masculinity, will atrophy and the benevolent tendencies will grow. 'Altruism' – Comte invented the word – will be the primary characteristic of Positivist man.

Taking the previous two ages of man as one – as the 'first life' of mankind – and the coming stage, the Positivist stage, as the second, we see that Comte thinks that the real problem with the first was the unbridled aggression which prevailed. In the new age we shall all be altruistic. So it seems that the Conservative wants nothing less than to change human nature. There is no disrespect or Freudianism in remarking here about the analogy between this supposed change in human nature and Comte's own life. His 'first career', which includes his common-law marriage to a prostitute and the elaboration of his intellectual system (the Aristotelian stage), is plainly analogous to the aggressive period in human history. His 'second career', with its sublimation of his passion for Madame de Vaux and the writing of his 'religious' works, corresponds to the altruistic life of man to come.[10]

The first thing Comte has to do to convince the Conservatives to put this programme into action is to recognize that feeling is prior to thought. Of the feelings which matter most, altruism is, of course, given a special place. If only all men would be altruistic, the present anarchy could be ended. This primacy of feeling over thought leads Comte to one of his central themes – the veneration of 'humanity'. The mere discovery of a positive science of sociology, important though it is, cannot control the future activity of men unless they can be brought to worship this new science. Hence the preparation of this new cult is one of the fundamental tasks of all Positivists. The artist, for example, is to play an important role by idealizing the future and so speeding the new day.[11]

Comte's choice of 'humanity' as an object of veneration is instructive for the light it throws on his whole way of thinking. He believed that a religion needed three elements – dogma, worship and government. He saw no difficulty in the object of veneration being a creation of men. He did not think that St Paul really believed in Christ and did not see why he should believe in humanity.[12] This is apparently one of the things meant by the priority of feeling over thought. He did not even claim that humanity was the highest entity in the solar system, and blandly admitted that future investigations might well discover some superior being. Although he claimed that he recognized the importance of the intellect, he deprived his 'humanity' of all those qualities which had made the Christian God intellectually presentable.

Comte criticizes the Christian conception of God, who is omniscient and wise, saying that it is foolish to commend an omniscient being for being wise. But the objection is trifling, and does nothing to diminish the Christian claim to a God who is worthy of veneration. The same can hardly be said for Comte's humanity. It appears that Comte's reason for choosing humanity as an object of veneration is the nice thought that men who worship humanity could not possibly go to war with each other. Altruism, it seems, is akin to docility.

All of these absurdities are compounded in Comte's writing. It is almost unbelievable that he was taken seriously at all; and yet he was. And it is the seriousness with which he was taken, the fact that large numbers of people actually believed his doctrines and set up schools to study them and propagate the message, which makes him of interest in this study. His work, as I have pointed out, is ideological in any sense of that term. It presents a view of humanity, a guide of action, a programme for the renovation of society, it is intolerant of opponents, rigid, it grossly overestimates the power of words, and it is obviously biased in favour of specific social classes. It did all this in a France which was not short of alternative ideologies : Socialism, Liberalism, Christianity, anarchism, monarchism and many others were in the air. The fact then that this absurd doctrine could be taken seriously against such competition points to the inescapable importance of ideology in that time and, by extension, in our time.

Comte sums up his entire programme in the maxim: 'Love, the principle, and Order for basis; Progress for end.'[13] This combination of order and progress, the Conservatives are assured, will enable them to overcome the difficulties inherent in both revolutionary and reactionary doctrines. The moment for the realization of these advances, they are forewarned, is at hand. Positive policy in regard to the reactionaries is to take the form of proposing a religious alliance. Comte wants the reactionaries to be shown that their present politics must inevitably fail because the Catholic religion upon which they are based is inadequate. The greatest weakness of the Church is its blindness to progress. Comte promises to conquer this disability and reassures the Conservatives and the reactionaries that history is inevitably on their side. The world, he says, 'becomes more and more religious'. Comte is confident that the reactionaries will readily adopt Positivism when they see that it brings stability.

The revolutionists present Comte with a different problem. He thinks that they have rightly perceived that the religious systems of the past were inadequate to human needs, and he praises them for having introduced new ontologies to meet the difficulty. He praises them also for having seen that only a systematic solution to the problems of man could expect to be successful. But the revolutionists' proposed solution is a bad one. Hence, Comte tells the Conservatives, the way to make allies of the revolutionists is to divide and conquer them. The revolutionists are already divided into two camps – teachers and followers : and Comte is confident that the followers can be led once the teachers are discredited. The Positivist is to discredit the revolutionary teachers by showing that they are little more than false prophets who would rule the proletariat against its true interests. Next, the Positivists must show the proletariat, hitherto the followers of the revolutionists, that Positivism is in their true interest. Together, they march under the slogan 'Live for Others'.

Comte foresees a situation in which the proletariat and the women are to become the two most important upholders of the new Positivist ideology. They are ideally suited for their new role, both by reason of their present discontent and their lack of education. The way Comte wants to win over these groups is to develop an acceptable ideology; no other persuasion is deemed necessary. He calls for 'the free elaboration of public opinion'. Thus fortified by a religious alliance with the reactionaries, a political alliance with the revolutionists and an ideological union with both, the Positivist hopes to have the authority to enact his programme.

Comte believes that if he begins immediately preparing the new cult and propagating for it, the new day will be prepared for 1 January 1900, which rounds things off neatly. Comte expects his Conservatives – industrialists, bankers, merchants and civil servants – to rule until 1900 and then docilely give up power to the newly educated Positivist priesthood. This abdication is manifestly the political analogue of the self-denial, even self-hatred, which Comte's altruism so clearly requires. He almost reduces man to self-denial. In the first place, reason is to be subject to the passions. Then the passions are to be radically restricted so that only altruism is given rein; the others are quashed. Finally, the race of altruistic men is to inherit the earth from the rest. In substance, then, Comte is completely opposite to the point of view expressed by Marx. Where Marx wants to create a society which will end human self-alienation, Comte wants to create one which will institutionalize alienation of a more severe kind than was even dreamed of by Marx.

In method, too, the two are opposed. Marx was ever conscious of the need to keep theory and practice, thought and deed on the same plane. Marx was also aware that a theory without political backing was worthless. Thus Marx's rhetoric is always designed to help the proletariat along a path it is travelling in any case. Marx's role is merely to articulate deeply felt feelings. But Comte's role is to create them *ex nihilo*. Thus despite his warnings against the usurpations of a philosophy not guided by science, he openly advocates tampering with the science when it suits his political purpose:

> Even in the simpler sciences perfect distinctness is impossible without overstepping the limits of actual proof. Still more, therefore, in Sociology will the conclusions of Science fall always far short of that degree of fullness, precision and clearness, without which no principles can be thoroughly popularised. But at the point where philosophy must always leave a void, poetry steps in and stimulates practical action.[14]

In these sentiments he shows himself to be an ideologist above all else. Indeed, surely we should count Comte and Positivism rather than Marx and Marxism as the paradigm of ideology.

# 8 Koestler's *Darkness at Noon*

## I

Lucien Goldmann, a French Marxist philosopher, propounds a fascinating analogy which leads to the suggestion that capitalism is a hero in a great world-historical tragedy.[1] The notion is worth pursuing. Surely capitalism has many of the characteristics of a tragic hero. It enters the stage of history fully worthy of respect; it is the successor to feudalism. It gains stature through the action of its own rich inner resources. It changes the face of the world. It comes to rule the world in a way no other has ever ruled it. Its needs are filled by the rape of the world's mineral resources. Morality, government and laws are ruthlessly brushed aside and changed to suit its whim. For all these reasons capitalism is worthy of our honour. For these reasons, too, it attracts our interest and wonder; it carries the mantle which the Greeks hung on their God-Men and the Christians on their Man-God. It is the primary object of awe in our culture.

Again, true to the model of a tragic hero, capitalism (on the Marxist reading) carries within it the seeds of its own inevitable destruction. Its own child, the proletariat, will rise up and smash his father. In place of the internal contradictions of an Oedipus, a Macbeth, we have the internal self-contradictions of capitalism. In place of the tragic flaw, the negation of the negation.

If we refrain from overdoing the analogy, it has considerable power. Capitalism is indeed *like* a tragic hero. But it is not ultimately the same thing. We must resist thinking them identical. Capitalism cannot literally *be* a tragic hero (from the Marxist point of view at least), for a tragic hero is the most dignified and powerful actor on the stage, and if this is allowed, what are we to say of the proletariat – not to mention Communism?

Not the least powerful part of Goldmann's analogy is the fact that it gives some clue to the charms of being a Communist. Communism seeks to guide the proletariat to the murder of capitalism and to rise the ruler of the era following. Thus to be a Communist is to have a role, a vital role, in world history. The mere act of joining the C.P. lifts one out of the terrible boredom of daily existence. Before joining, one is oppressed – or, worse, an oppressor; now one is Prometheus. To kill this hero, this king among heroes – that is a job worth doing. It is to touch, even to become part of, the magic of history.

Marx's description of capitalism, most powerfully in the *Communist Manifesto,* is in harmony with Goldmann's analogy. His respect for the historical power of capitalism is unmistakable; as, too, in his belief that its own internal contradictions will bring it down. Finally, Marx accords a great place in this history drama to the Communist Party. Perhaps, then, Goldmann is drawing our attention to, or is making explicit and conscious for the first time, an internal drama which has long served to draw men to Communism.

It would be hard to overestimate the power of this commitment once it has been entered into, and an explanation of its genesis is certainly called for. Towards this cause, in order fully to play a role in this drama, large numbers of seemingly moderate and reasonable men have willingly, even joyously, devoted their lives. Some have gone even further, made their lives a sacrifice to the cause – jumped, as it were, into the fire of history. And in so doing, have they not made a tragic metaphor of themselves? In dying as part of a historical drama, their actions acquire – or at least aspire to – a dignity which their humdrum existence could not otherwise hope to match. In this context, one's own death passes beyond being something to be feared and becomes almost something to be embraced.

In these respects too, the analogy has power. One prerequisite of tragedy was a willingness to face death with nobility: to face it with dignity as part of the role of life. The ideal tragic hero, Milton's Samson Agonistes for instance, gains in stature at his death as part of the price of freeing his people from bondage and of redeeming his own name. His death, the death of any tragic hero, always foreseen by the audience, brings down the curtain on a drama when the action is complete. This completeness adds to the satisfaction of the play. It is of a piece. Thus the hero must die. But were his death the result of chance, or accident, or were he unwilling to accept it, the audience would be cheated. The crucial *catharsis* of which Aristotle speaks as the result of tragedy would be absent. One would leave the theatre thinking 'if only he hadn't . . .'. But this is what we constantly say of our own actions. Tragedy charms by raising its hero – and its audience by an act of identification – above the level of the mundane. *We* seek to escape death at all costs, and when we are honest with ourselves we admit this; thus we admire the tragic hero for actually being what we wish to be when he escapes from the fear of death.

Notoriously, however, bourgeois man, man in the dull repetitive cycle of life in the city, ignores this aristocratic ideal. Bourgeois man is Hobbesian man, frightened of a violent death more than anything else in the world. This man is the slave of any who credibly threatens his life. He is unfit to perform heroic actions. 'Bravery' is mistaken by him for foolhardiness. This man has obviously forgotten his God. He will ignore the promise of a sweet life after death. He will ignore any story or charm which seeks to assuage his fear lest it tempt him to throw away or treat lightly what is most precious to him – his life. In bourgeois society, tragedy will give way to some other kind of literature. It will give way so that the basic mythical tales it relates are less and less seriously believed; and it will give way as the morality it embodies becomes a source of embarrassment or even of threat.

Both of these prerequisites are restored by the Communist view of capitalism which Goldmann voices. In *Darkness at Noon*, Arthur Koestler undertakes the formidable task of disenchanting the Communist view of its drama. He writes *Darkness at Noon* to woo men out of the party and to warn others away. How this is attempted, and how much success he has at it – at using fiction for ideological purposes – is the subject of this chapter.

## II

The works of ideology so far considered in this section have been written speeches, pamphlets and appeals. None of them was a work of fiction. Perhaps at first glance it may seem a little strange to rank *Darkness at Noon* along with *Areopagitica*, *Common Sense* and *Appeal to Conservatives*. For one thing, many of the rhetorical techniques used by the earlier authors have been so over-used by the mid-twentieth century that they are in disrepute. In Koestler's work the words, which might have been uttered by Paine or Comte, 'Experience teaches, that the masses must be given for all difficult and complicated processes a simple, easily grasped explanation',[2] are put into the mouth a 'Neanderthal' tormentor of the hero. Time has passed the simpler techniques by. For another thing, the author of a novel or, even more, a play, has a problem of 'voice' which a non-fiction author escapes.

We can never unguardedly assume that the sentiments put by an author into the mouth of one of his actors, even his hero, are his own sentiments. We cannot, for example, assume, as some English chauvinists would have us do, that John of Gaunt speaks for Shakespeare when he praises England; we remember how ungrateful England is to this patriot. For another thing, long arguments and political programmes do not fit easily into a novel. Some novelists – Huxley in *Eyeless in Gaza*, for example – are often criticized for making their novels the creatures of their philosophies.

But these problems are not insuperable and have been successfully resolved by various authors. One thinks immediately of Zola's *Germinal* where the main ideological themes are repeated endlessly. Even so, the book has a remarkable power and hardly seems adversely affected at all. If Zola solves the problem of repetition, Dickens solves many others. His works have a manifest political punch while forsaking nothing in characterization or plot. In this century, Orwell wrote compellingly in *1984* to warn against total state control; and Huxley in *Brave New World* more successfully points to the price of freedom in a technologically sophisticated society. But if the problems of reconciling fiction and ideology have, from time to time, been overcome, they are still real enough. It still takes some skill to turn these problems to advantage. *Darkness at Noon* passes this test.

Koestler is helped, of course, by the mood of the day. The novel appeared in 1941 at a time when Britain was fighting in alliance with the Soviet Union against Nazi Germany. It appeared, thus, in a world which was alive to – if slightly confused by – ideology. The traumatic turnabouts in Soviet foreign policy, its siding against Fascism, then with Germany, then against it again, were still fresh in the public eye. The extraordinary convolutions of logic which British Communists accepted at the command of

Moscow were there for all to see, and the public recantations of ex-Communists, Koestler among them, were general knowledge. All this conduces at once to make a rhetoric of ideology, most especially Communist ideology, part of the culture of the time and the object at once of wonder and not a little fear. Thus much of the tiresome repetitive exhortation and explanation which an ideologist – like the author of the *Communist Manifesto* – must engage in, is unnecessary. Ideology, in the mid-twentieth century, is part of the public vocabulary. There is no need for Koestler to teach it anew. If ideology, in this case the myth of capitalism and its titanic clash with Promethean Communism, does not entirely replace religion as the central myth of the day, it at least established itself as its co-equal.

Thirty years later, in the 1970s, we can see these ideological myths surpass religion in this respect, so much so that the official champions of Christianity sue for peace. Surely this is the real meaning of the Christian–Marxist dialogue. The older partner seeks to gain a last regeneration by adopting the rhetoric and stance of its younger, infinitely more virile brother. But here we get ahead of ourselves; the point is that novelists and playwrights in our time can freely adopt the conventions and mythical stories of ideology without having to repeat the whole story, just as earlier writers could adopt the myths and rhetoric of Christianity. This simplifies the task of some ideologists enormously, while at the same time making it increasingly difficult for others who wish to speak outside these conventions.

*Darkness at Noon* records several days in the life of Nicholas Salmanovitch Rubashov. Rubashov, formerly one of the leaders of the Revolution, is in jail for the final time. He has committed crimes against the state, or rather – if indeed it is rather – against the Leader, against Number One. Rubashov is to be killed by the state apparatus, but it would first be ever so much more convenient if he would confess to the false accusations.

It would always be a simple enough matter for his murder to be arranged as an administrative matter. Rubashov is rarely in any doubt that this is the only alternative available to him.[3] He can die in silence having retained his dignity; or he can comply with the last wishes of the Party, sign a false confession and admit all in open court, and then die. Despite the fact that he sees the alternatives clearly, he chooses to oblige the Party. He confesses.

In this, at least, Rubashov is the arch-antihero. He turns down his chance for a noble death – to die in silence – and chooses to be of service to the end. Rubashov is Comrade Rubashov to the end. He serves the Party, not himself. To be a hero, to retain one's dignity, is to stand on one's own, to be an individual.

Rubashov has long since abdicated this part. Even the years of public adulation during which he was one of the ruling three have not changed his mind. His face, once familiar to all, for his portrait is on every house in a place of honour and still familiar to the older generation, is not turned by temporary success. To the end, he will not detract from the Party by standing out against it. His confession to crimes he never dreamed of committing is wanted because, despite his recent eclipse, he is still respected by many. His confession will serve to reconcile those who trust him and remember him as the last important member of the older generation to Number One. In this play Prometheus will stand no upstaging.

The confession is made freely because Rubashov realizes that he has gone too far to oppose the wishes of the Party now. He knows all the arguments against the logic of the Party all too well; he has used them himself in the service of the Party. Through a series of memories, Koestler shows us Rubashov in his role of Party official.

We see Comrade Rubashov urge the Communist dock workers in a hostile capitalist country to break their own boycott against shipments to a Fascist country. This is done in order to let a shipment of arms from the mother-country go through to the Fascists. The short-term interests of the Party and the country are made paramount. In order that the Revolution does not suffer there, it is to be betrayed everywhere else.

We are never told that the mother-country is Russia; that the Fascist country is Spain; that the Party is the Communist Party; that Rubashov is part of the great show trials of the 1930s; or that Stalin is putting into effect his doctrine of 'Socialism in one country'. These fact are conveyed by allusion. In this case the allusive, abstract, colourless character of the betrayed of non-Soviet Communist Parties and the proletariat is oddly suited to the dream-like memories in which Rubashov recalls them. By putting such events into this form, Koestler heightens his main themes: we see Rubashov as a shadowy figure. He is a man reduced by his ideological allegiances to a wasted shell. All that is left of him is his dialectical skill. The thinness of his humanity is suited to these twice removed mental images. What we hear is a voice in a memory in the thought processes of a condemned man.

Pathetically, even these memories are a comfort to Rubashov. They take his mind off his awful toothache – shrewd touch that, what could be so infuriatingly obtrusive as a throbbing toothache? – and give him what little solace he can find. We see this clearly in Rubashov's reflections on his lover Arlova. Even the sensuousness of their love-making is reduced to a mental image; and as she is now an image in Party history (he betrayed her in order to go on working for the Party), so she was once a useful secretary in Party work. Even his love is part of his ideology. Thus Koestler builds up an image in the readers of the contorted, inhumane life of Party members.

His claim has two faces: in the first place he shows through Rubashov that Party work requires the sacrifice of all the things his audience calls virtuous – love, family, friendship, humour and life; and on the other, he claims that the supposed honour and glamour of working for a just cause is chimerical.[4] Of the first group, greatest play is made with the last two mentioned. Rubashov is a comrade of the older generation of comrades, one of whom is his final tormentor. The specific difference between his generation and the present generation of Neanderthals who have inherited the Revolution Rubashov's contemporaries made, is humour. The Neanderthals are such earnest brutes they cannot laugh at themselves. 'The most conspicuous trait of the Neanderthal character was its absolute humourlessness, or, more exactly, its lack of frivolity.'[5] If this is not warning enough, there is always the nice prospect – actualized in Rubashov's case – of an unjust death.

The illogicality and ruthlessness of Party work is reiterated throughout the book. I have already mentioned the betrayal of Communist dockers in an unfriendly country. There is the equally effective memory of the day Rubashov had to make contact with a young comrade in another foreign country. The home country was not pleased by the acolyte's efforts. His cell had been clandestinely distributing news-sheets which told the truth about the Party's failures in that country. The Party line dictated that hopes and enthusiasm be maintained. The workers must be told that the Party is gathering strength at the very time it was smashed by the local police. The young comrade could not accept this – as Rubashov well knew in advance, since the young comrade's girl friend had been informing on him to the Party – so Rubashov casts him out of the Party and into the grasp of the local police. Warning enough?

The point is driven home most tellingly against Rubashov during his first interview in jail. He is asked to explain his actions and he utters a 'grammatical fiction': he distinguishes between 'I' and 'we', between himself and the Party. This is the basic error for which he is now made to pay.

In making this payment so high, Koestler makes his own ideological point – for none could deny that this novel is a move in an ideological game. He warns against the ideologists' way of life in terms of stark simplicity. In this, Koestler is working a venerable literary genre. This work recalls – but does it match up to? – Plato's warnings in the *Republic* (the myth of Er) against the way of life of the politician. This resonance enables us, I think, to brush aside complaints that *Darkness at Noon* is an inferior novel for its obsession with ideology. Irving Howe makes this complaint in *Politics and the Novel*, but in so doing he misses one of Koestler's most effective points: that ideology disfigures the lives of those who take it too seriously.[6] By demonstrating the truth of this point, Koestler has also overridden whatever remaining doubts there may be about the use of fiction as a vehicle for ideology. The use can be effective ideology and good fiction.

## III

The title of Koestler's work recalls Milton's tragedy *Samson Agonistes*; yet the two works are not obviously similar. Koestler's title brings to mind Samson's lament. Samson, blinded, betrayed, weakened, enslaved by the enemies of his people, is 'eyeless in Gaza'. Samson is almost the perfect tragic hero and Milton's poem is nearly perfect tragedy according to the Aristotelian canon.[7] Samson, proud hero of his people, is introduced by a chorus of Hebrews. He has been brought down through his own pride. His pride led him to think he was so much better than normal men that he was exempt from the prohibitions of moral law. One of these prohibitions forbade Jews from marrying Gentiles. Samson broke the taboo when he married Delilah. He pays the price of his *hubris* when Delilah betrays him to her people, the enemies of his people. He ought to have expected as much, but was blinded by his pride; now he is literally blind:

> O dark, dark, dark, amid the blaze of noon,
> Irrecoverably dark, total eclipse
> Without all hope of day.[8]

In the end, again true to the model of an Aristotelian tragedy, Samson regains stature (if not sight) when he redeems himself by killing all the Gentiles.

Rubashov's fate is quite different. It is central to Koestler's intention that it remain so. Rubashov must be broken completely by Communism if his story is to suit Koestler's main themes. Thus Rubashov's tale is a plunge from arrest through imprisonment to death, unrelieved throughout the book save by a few ethereal memories. While such a story line might conceivably make theatre, it cannot be tragedy.

Even on the somewhat less precise standard of drama, *Darkness at Noon* would be difficult to do effectively. The other characters, even Rubashov's two inquisitors, appear in the tale only as part of Rubashov's fight with the Party. They remain figments of his illogical demise; they never become characters in their own right. For this reason too, drama will not do.

On the other hand, all these factors are no disadvantage to the novelist. They appear as contingencies, but in fact *Darkness at Noon* makes a good novel for reasons that point to the usefulness of the novel for ideological work in general. It is hardly a contingent fact about *Darkness at Noon* that it concerns the private life and decisions of a citizen. These things are characteristic of the novels of our time, and are useful to the ideologist because he is concerned to shift the opinions and decisions of such private men.[9]

As Rubashov thinks out his fate in private, so we read novels in private, and so too we vote in private. The secret ballot, keystone of the mythology of democracy, is meant to be sacred largely because it is private. We consider men's private actions to be their true and important actions. We have convinced ourselves that a man is most himself 'in the privacy of his home'. An older tradition, a tradition of a culture in which drama was rich and even philosophy occurred in dialogues, held that men were their best in public. An illustration of an action from this older tradition helps to make the point: when Brutus and Antony address the Roman mob come to bury Ceasar, they also address us the audience. By being there in the same room with the mob, we understand the speeches, and their reactions to them, far more vividly than we would if we read them to ourselves at home. The actions which determine who is to follow Ceasar take place in public and are best rehearsed on stage, in public. Rubashov does not make speeches, neither is he part of a mob. He is alone in the quiet of his thoughts and we are also alone when we read the novel.

The novel is the appropriate form of fiction for taking an ideological message to a literate middle-class audience. Since this is the audience which can identify with Rubashov and the audience which, in 1941 at least, dominated politics, an ideologist must speak to them. It may well be, of course, that as our society becomes increasingly proletarian, other forms of literature will supersede the novel. Perhaps this is what the street theatre movement is all about.

It is certainly the case that classical drama had a political role and a form which was suited to a polity ruled, alternately, by mobs and oligarchs. Tragedy was the dramatic tool of the oligarch – 'aristocrats' as they would have it. In tragedy, the hero had a dignity flattering to the aristocrats' self-image. Moreover, in a successful tragedy the conventional order of things is reaffirmed. The hero is struck down for daring to break the moral law and is restored to dignity only when he redeems himself. Moreover, the effect of the whole is cathartic: dangerous passions, envy and ambition are harmlessly drained.

Comedy, on the other hand, was the friend of the mob – 'democrats' as would be. In Aristophanes's plays, Socrates is made the fool. Plato returns the compliment in his comedy *The Symposium*. Aristophanes is seen to be such a weak-minded lover of poetry that he cannot even stay awake long enough to hear the speech which shows the unity of tragedy and comedy. In comedy, the highbrow, the noble and the dignified are brought down. To use Bergson's splendid image, they slip on banana peels. In comedy, pretence and convention are moved and ridiculed. The arch formality which is the essence of rank cannot stand here.

But neither of these conventions will do in a polity of private individuals. What is left to them must be encapsulated into the novel. *Darkness at Noon* is neither tragedy nor, despite its appeal to humour, is it very funny. There are, of course, contemporary dramas which have an ideological point – Anouilh's *Antigone* and Sartre's *No Exit*, to name two. But in a culture in which theatre-going is the prerogative of the sophisticated few, a novel can reach a larger audience and thus have greater effect.


## IV


The ideological effect a novel can have will depend, of course, on the political situation in which its readers live. Censorship difficulties to the side for a moment, one can imagine that *Darkness at Noon* would have had quite a different effect – a different ideological meaning in fact – in the Soviet Union.

Ideological as well as merely political works have sometimes had an effect different from that intended, or even conceived of, by their authors. Plato, suitably expurgated to be sure, was required reading in Nazi schools according to Professor Popper. But then one remembers that the Devil can quote scripture – and one is grateful suddenly that God is not quite dead.

This danger, or advantage, is more likely to befall the writer of ideological fiction than that of non-fiction. Koestler's novel contains mere allusions to the Soviet Union and Communism. It never mentions the name of any historical person. These allusions are useful to Koestler, for specific references to actual people and actual incidents would date the novel quickly as well as blunt its point. The criticism is of ideology and its creations, not specifically of Stalinism. Post-Stalinist Soviet leaders may try to throw off the stigma of Stalinism, but Koestler's images dog them.

In some respects, *Darkness at Noon* looks like being a fictional part of the anti-totalitarian literature which was so popular in American political science and philosophy after the Second World War.[10] But the book was published during (from the American point of view, before) the war and, more impressively still, it endures when books like Friedrich and Brzezinski's *Totalitarian Dictatorship and Autocracy* are now so obviously dated products of a past era.[11] *Darkness at Noon* can be read with point in more various places than the more explicit, less nimble, descriptive literature which has much the same message.

It is interesting in this respect briefly to mention Alexander Solzhenitsyn's prison novels: *A Day in the Life of Ivan Denisovich* and *First Circle*. Despite the similarity of locale, neither of these books is at all like *Darkness at Noon*. Solzhenitsyn's novels show people in camps. Their situation is very much part of the novels and yet the ideological punch – the condemnation of a whole order of society – is missing.

In *Darkness at Noon* we are made constantly aware of the moral of the tale. The irony of Rubashov's reflections on his loyalty forces that moral into our minds. In *First Circle*, however, and even interestingly in *Ivan Denisovich*, we are aware of a human condition. Lukács has observed, correctly I think, that the real interest of *Ivan Denisovich* rests in the sheer struggle for life.[12] The details of his daily life, his struggle for warmth and food, are so overwhelming that Ivan has no time – and his readers no cause – to reflect on the 'larger' ideological issues.

These ideological issues seem, from the point of view of this novella, at once the luxury of comfortable, well-fed intellectuals, and again ultimately trivial when compared to the really profound things. Ivan uses every nerve in this one day's struggle to stay alive and preserve his self-respect. Our attention is rarely relieved from his day by memories of the world beyond the camp. The struggle here is enough. Towards the end of the day Ivan recalls that he wrote to his wife asking her not to send him food parcels any longer. Her struggle is hard too. She does not need any additional burdens. To each his own Hell.

Where Koestler's Rubashov reflects on the bright world beyond the past, he heightens our awareness of what ideology has cost him. In Ivan's life there is only a choice – and it most certainly is not his choice but that of a blind system – between kinds of Hell. One might say that Ivan has a 'falsely conscious' view of his world, that he thinks only of himself, ignoring the wider political implications, but for the fact that he patently has no consciousness at all.

Since the novelist produces his impact by focusing the reader's sympathy on his central characters, and Ivan lacks any conscious-ness, this novella is devoid of ideology. This cannot be said of the central prisoner in *First Circle*. These men are all first-class scientists, many of whom know of the kind of camp in which Ivan survives. They have been singled out for special treatment like the prisoners in the first circle of Dante's inferno. They know that their relative comfort is granted in order to allow them to complete a voice-identification machine which the government wants.

Their efforts are thus frantic, and not a little comic. But they are not for all that ideological figures. Their innocence of ideology is maintained in two ways. Firstly, as in *Ivan Denisovich*, Solzhenitsyn paints a picture of the frustrations of civilian life so infuriating in its awkwardness that the contrast with prison life is poignant. This time one has two kinds of purgatory – and always everyone is aware of the proximity of Hell. Secondly, ideology is kept out of the book by Solzhenitsyn's splendid portrait of Stalin – the man who all know is directing everything. Stalin emerges in *First Circle* as a restless, unhappy, anguished man. He is a man for all his power. Solzhenitsyn gives the man his name; Koestler keeps him at a distance, calls him 'Number One'. The difference neatly summarizes the difference between their works in this respect.

Solzhenitsyn's character is a human being, as pitiable as any prisoner: Koestler's character is an ideological creation, a nexus of dialectical intercourse. Solzhenitsyn's Stalin is pitiable, and with this touch a whole system is made human. One cannot hate a man; one certainly cannot if one is the humane, moderate, civilized man to whom *Darkness at Noon* is addressed.

Solzhenitsyn has written some ideological short stories – *For the Good of the Cause* is an obvious example. Here all the down-trodden are innocent pleasant people who bend to the whim of bureaucratic dictate. The bureaucrats, on the other hand, are selfish, careerist officials who think only of their next promotion and who never, never, break the rules. But such stick figures are absent from his prison works and the ideological effect is missing too. That actual Soviet officials, like the stick figures he portrays, think all Solzhenitsyn's work ideological only reaffirms the point.

## V

Marx likened the proletariat to Prometheus. Goldmann likens capitalism to a tragic hero. The two images can be combined. Prometheus steals fire from the older generation of gods and gives industry to man. The proletariat learns all from capitalism and uses its knowledge to overcome its parent-tyrant. But who is to speak for the proletariat and who for capitalism? Koestler assumes that the Communist Party speaks for the proletariat. In our age, a concern with social justice is almost identical with at least a flirtation with Communism. But need this be so? *Darkness at Noon* bids us look elsewhere. But where? On this the book gives us no clue; and in that, it is a failure. But perhaps the failure is not Koestler's alone. What, after all, are the alternatives? What other role can one play?

# Part 3
# The Political Use of Ideology

# 9 Marxism

There should be little question that the Marxist movement in all its various shapes is *the* social and political doctrine of our age. There are exceptions to this rule, of course, and there are divisions in the Marxist camp to be sure; but to a remarkable degree the serious political ideas of our day are either pro-Marxist or anti-Marxist. Whether one prefers the opinion of Professor Acton that Marxism is the illusion of the epoch, or Professor Aron's similar view that it is the opium of the intellectuals, or Sartre's opposite view that it is the philosophy of our time, the fact of its pre-eminence is hardly in dispute.[1] Whether one is pro- or anti-Marxist, the terms of one's social rhetoric, the force of moral suasion, is likely to be dictated by some series of ideas derived, however clumsily, from Marx.

We may think this a pity, we may wish for a less old-fashioned, less rigid, less muddled point of view, we may, most of all, wish for something different; but the fact remains, certainly as concerns any idea which has an audience outside universities, that Marxism commands the centre of the field. The other two ideologies which I shall comment on in this section, Liberalism and Conservatism, are today, as shall be argued, primarily reactions against the progeny of Marxism.

In his recent book *Against the Self-Images of the Age*, Alasdair MacIntyre has, in effect, disputed this assertion.[2] He believes that Marxism co-exists with Christianity and psychoanalysis as the major ideologies of the age. Against this, one can only repeat the opinion stated in Chapter 8, that the kind of Christianity which prospers in our world is a very much mutilated thing. In this opinion I am more in agreement with the teaching of MacIntyre's earlier book *Marxism and Christianity*, that the Christianity which survives most heartily in our own time is very much a

Marxist Christianity.[3] It seems to me that those Christians whose teachings strike a responsive chord in contemporary men are precisely those who, like Ivan Illich and the worker priests, teach a Gospel so radically social and, moreover, socially egalitarian and revolutionary, as to be indistinguishable from the students of the so-called early Marx.[4] Hence I cannot accept MacIntyre's opinion that Christianity co-exists with Marxism as a separate moral force.

Psychoanalysis is another matter; no less so for the attempts of Herbert Marcuse to combine it with Marxism. Neither do I wish to deny that the psychoanalytic movement presents an image of man which is unique and valuable, or that it is widespread (though patchily so; it is more popular in the intellectual society of the north-eastern United States than in most other places), but I am not aware that it has produced more than a sketchy and incoherent social philosophy. Moreover, it has not produced a distinctive view of ideology. And indeed, I take MacIntyre's own relative silence on the subject of psychoanalysis's 'self-image' – and his total silence on the matter of its social image – as confirmation of this shortcoming.

It might also be objected that nationalism is a popular sentiment in the modern world, and that it is neither specifically pro- nor anti-Marxist.[5] I accept this objection as far as it goes. Nationalism is currently widespread and recurrent in our world. But surely it is really more of a sentiment than a theory or a point of view, a sentiment which takes a variety of different forms – Conservative, Liberal or Marxist – according to circumstances. Also, the various nationalisms are necessarily opposed to one another. English nationalism and Scottish nationalism have little enough in common. They are necessarily opposed in a way which makes it difficult to accept that there is any underlying theory involved. The various branches of Marxism are also opposed, as the gleeful accounts of numerous unsympathetic observers have attested, but theirs is a family quarrel: a bitter quarrel at times, but one which serves ultimately only to remind one how much they really do have in common.

## II

Marxism in our time takes two forms. It is either philosophical – the heir to the intellectual tools used by Marx in his youthful writings – or it is political, heir to the notion that the achievement of Communism via a working-class revolution is the paramount aim.[6] Philosophical Marxism is, by itself, a most virile social philosophy; it has deeply influenced European social thought and, via the New Left and the so-called 'Marxist–Christian' dialogue, is important in Britain and the United States. The main theoretical interest of this school is the concept of alienation. It is concerned to show, as was Marx, that modern society destroys the souls of its citizens and is concerned to plot out the available alternatives. Marcuse, Ivan Illich, Shlomo Avineri and George Lichtheim are, in their very separate ways, part of this movement. Philosophical Marxism is not impressed with the notion that a proletarian revolution could end alienation, nor does it, generally, much concern itself with the pretenders to Marx's political heritage. It is certainly not convinced that life is better, in any important way, in the Soviet countries.

Political Marxism takes a very different view. It is much more inclined to take seriously the entire body of Marx's work and to play down the importance of the earlier works. Isaac Deutscher, until his recent death, was a massively eloquent exponent of this point of view. Deutscher, even after his expulsion from the Polish Communist Party by the Stalinists in 1932, remained very much a Communist. He never wavered in his belief in the primacy of the class struggle and the ultimate victory of the proletariat. Not all political Marxists are that committed. But they all retain – and this I take to be the hallmark of political Marxism – a belief that society is basically a class struggle, that no one or thing is neutral in this struggle and that everything must be known by its place in the context of this struggle. This leads us straight on to ideology: an ideology, to a political Marxist, is the intellectual tool of the opposition class. But before we come to consider that idea, one or two caveats are necessary.

When I speak of political Marxists, I have in mind people like Deutscher, Nigel Harris and Lenin. None of these writers accepts the full weight of political Marxism; each makes at least one important deviation from the basic theory. Harris, for example, holds that the real struggle is no longer between rich and poor within a nation, but between the rich and poor nations. Most important, each accepts the primacy of struggle. They are all inclined to castigate as 'Liberal' any denial of this primacy. In speaking of political Marxism, one is then speaking of a school, of like-minded writers pursuing a common theme in various ways.

The other caveat follows closely from this: Marxism is not a static body of doctrine. This fact emerges clearly from Lichtheim's *Marxism: An Historical and Critical Study*.[7] Lichtheim observes that Marxism has, in effect, split into two – a theory and a practice. The practice – what takes place under the name of Socialism in the Soviet bloc – can retain no claim to the philosophical underpinning which set the Marxist movement going in the first place. The practice has become, in effect, the Russian way to bureaucracy in an industrialized country. It has nothing to do with Marxist aspirations for a classless society.[8] The theory of Marxism, on the other hand, is a mere abstraction; the history of the Marxist movement has shown it to be unrealizable. It is abstract in precisely the way Hegel's political philosophy was. But Marxism was meant to be a fusion of theory and practice. To say that the two are separate is to say that classical Marxism is dead. Thus the Marxism which lives in our world must be a development from its source.

In stating that the Soviet practice has failed – and in acknowledging that that practice is the legitimate heir to Marx's practical efforts – Lichtheim speaks for all contemporary Marxists (with the unimportant exception of the following of the Fourth International), be they philosophically or politically inclined. Our Marxists disagree about which part of the theory is worth pursuing – the theory of human nature and alienation, or the theory of class struggle – but they agree in finding the Soviet example an embarrassment. Both schools call on exigetical advice to show that 'their' Marx is the real Marx. While it would be satisfying to be certain just what Marx meant in each work and to know how the various works relate to one another – and certainly scholars like Shlomo Avineri and David McLellan (both of whom are sympathetic to the philosophical school) have performed useful service in this regard – these exigetical questions are not really crucial here.[9] The fact is that both schools are developing Marx's ideas. Something new is emerging; something not present in, though plainly inspired by, Marx. The puzzling thing for us, however, is that these contemporary theorists are not developing Marx's concept of idealogy.

# III

As I have shown in the first part of this book, Marx had two different things in mind when he spoke of ideology. A theory could be ideological because it advanced an incoherent or incomplete view. Classical political economy was ideological in this sense. Adam Smith, for all his honest scientific endeavour, did not – could not – see society from the final perspective available to Marx. A writing was also ideological if it deliberately distorted the truth in order to advance partisan interest. Malthus, a vulgar economist, was an ideologist in this sense. The first notion, where ideology is synonymous with false consciousness, historically precedes the latter.

Much, if not all, post-Marx Marxist thinking is bedevilled by the failure to make this distinction. Marx is often taken, by his champions and heirs, to be stating that all ideology is false consciousness. It is not. Nevertheless, the notion of ideology as false consciousness is manifestly the more interesting and important of the two notions. Most of us, most of the time, speak from limited views of events. We see things from our private vantage-points first, and best. There is nothing especially narrow or mean about this. It is just a fact of life. Those who have the gifts of sympathy and intelligence and the leisure to listen to others might overcome the limits of their own position. But few people are so gifted. The rest of us will be falsely conscious. We will not see that our perspective is narrow; we will not realize that we are being unfair to others. Thus when we speak of our hopes and fears, we will clothe them in the garb of right. We will be stating our selfish interest to be right. This is what is meant by false consciousness. In Marx's terms, we are stating our ideology. Since he assumes that most bourgeois men think immediately of their position in class terms – they think of themselves immediately as members of the middle class – their ideology is always a function of their class. This process, an innocent arrogance, is surely the more common position. The self-consciously malevolent – those who deliberately overlook the claims of others – the cynics, are, I suspect, rather few. Both the innocent and the malevolent speak from self-interest though they claim to speak of the general interest; thus they look to the outsider as much the same. In virtue of this similarity, they can

both be called ideologists. We may say that there are many roads
to ideology.

I say *many* roads where Marx knew *two*; is this not eclectic? I
think not. Marx knew two – one characteristic of each of the
major periods of bourgeois history. But Marx is long dead. Much
has happened to bourgeois thinking since his death. Is one not in
step with the major themes of his work if one suggests that bourgeois thinking – still the enemy of proletarian aspirations – has
acquired new forms? This point seems to me elementary. Marxist
thought (in the West at least) has failed to grasp it.[10] In fact,
instead of grasping this elemental point, contemporary Marxists
have only muddled Marx's two ideas together and failed to
develop his ideas about ideology in any real way.

Lichtheim's otherwise rather useful essay 'The Concept of
Ideology' and his remarks on ideology in a discussion published in
*Slavic Review* (March 1965), in response to the notions of Daniel
Bell, exhibit some confusion on this point.[11] The fact that Bell can
so easily ridicule Lichtheim in his response points to the weakness
of Lichtheim's position. Since this discussion, especially Lichtheim's part in it, throws much light on Marxist ideas on ideology
in general, it is worth considering at some length.

—   Bell thinks of ideologies as systems of ideas which serve to
'concretise' social values. Following Parsons, Bell believes that all
societies need ideologies and that they are all equally successful.
He does not want to judge between the various ideologies; merely
to describe their general features and functions in society. As I
have argued in Chapter 4, this approach to ideology raises
innumerable problems, not least that one may well doubt that
such systems of ideas exist in the minds of all the members of any
one society.

✓   Lichtheim cannot allow Bell's notion that all these 'ideologies'
are morally equal. He condemns Bell as a 'social relativist'. Lichtheim, following Marx, distinguishes between ideology – the ideas
of the others – and science, our ideas (his reasons for so doing are
examined below). Bell is able to push Lichtheim into a corner by
quoting Lenin (in *What Is to Be Done?*), using his rather than
Lichtheim's procedure.[12]

Lenin's statement arises in the context of a criticism of some of
his Social Democratic opponents. He attacks economism (roughly,
the notion that political action on behalf of the proletariat is

unnecessary because the internal contradictions of capitalism are so great that the revolution will come when economic conditions dictate) and the related belief that, at the appropriate moment, the workers will throw off their masters spontaneously. This is a dispute within the Marxist movement. Lenin's position is that economism and the spontaneity theories are naïve. They ignore the fact that the workers (like every other class) require leaders and the fact that the Russian workers (as well, for that matter, as the English and German workers), at that time (1902), were barely class-conscious and certainly not revolutionary. It is necessary, Lenin urges, to fight the enemy with their own weapons: with a party and a theory. Moreover, there can be only one party and one theory which speaks for the workers. What to call the theory of the workers? Lenin, to Lichtheim's subsequent embarrassment, calls it an ideology. He does so several times:

> Since there can be no talk of an independent ideology formulated by the working classes themselves, in the process of their movement, the *only* choice is – either bourgeois or socialist ideology. There is no middle course (for mankind has not created a 'third' ideology, and, moreover, in a society torn by class antagonisms, there can never be a non-class or above-class ideology). Hence to belittle the socialist ideology *in any way, to turn aside from it in the slightest degree*, means to strengthen bourgeois ideology. . . .[13] Even now the German working class is, so to speak, split up among a number of ideologies.[14]

In this context, Lenin's procedure is an intelligible thing for a Marxist to do. Lichtheim denies this. He tries to dismiss Lenin's remarks as 'a misuse of a terminology which as a Marxist he might have been expected to treat more carefully. It has no theoretical roots, but evidently springs from the pressing preoccupations of a political activist concerned with spreading the faith'.[15] This attempted dismissal is quite unnecessary. Lenin's remarks are easily defended as an extrapolation from Marx's ideas to fit a new situation. In calling Marxism an ideology, Lenin merely calls attention to the fact – central to his argument in *What Is to Be Done?* – that the workers need a theory to lead them in just the way that the bourgeois do. Bell grasps this point; Lichtheim fudges it. Why? Because Lichtheim insists on wedding 'false consciousness' to 'ideology' in the mistaken belief that such a wedding was central to Marx's concept of ideology and a mistaken notion that a Marxist dare not change anything in the sacred — texts. In effect, he is saying that Marx saw all ideology as the product of false consciousness. This is simply not true.


## IV

Philosophical and political Marxists think of ideology in terms which suit their concerns. Each of them emphasizes a different aspect of Marx's teaching. Philosophical Marxists are inclined to emphasize the 'false consciousness' aspect of the theory. Political Marxists are inclined to emphasize the function of ideas, especially the enemy's ideas, in a class struggle. Neither completely sorts the matter out, but the tendency to emphasize one or the other aspect is real enough.

Lichtheim's essay, 'The Concept of Ideology', is the best example of the more philosophically inclined Marxists' ideas. Speaking of ideology, Lichtheim observes 'that a propensity so widespread as the duplication and distortion of reality in thought lends itself to the historical process'.[16] Marx is cited as authorizing this notion:

> What Marx meant appears plainly enough from the *Theses on Feuerbach*, where the latter is blamed for not having carried through to the end his inversion of Hegel's system. He says, for example: 'Feuerbach sets out from the fact of religious self-alienation, the duplication of the world into a religious and secular one. . . . But the fact that the secular basis deserts its own sphere and establishes an independent realm in the clouds, can only be explained by the cleavage and self-contradiction within the secular basis.'[17]

Weber is allowed to have developed the concept by sharpening the distinction between ideology in this sense and ideology in the sense — of 'the thinking characteristic of the age'. That latter sense troubles Lichtheim, as his remarks on Mannheim show. Mannheim is said merely to have tried unsuccessfully to refute Georg Lukács, the Hungarian Marxist.[18]

Mannheim's relativism, his unwillingness to distinguish between ideology and truth, is criticized by Lichtheim. Mannheim is said to have abandoned philosophy (I take this to mean that he is un-willing to state a view of final truth). Hence Lichtheim wishes to play down the notion of ideology as 'the thinking characteristic of the age', because that notion is neutral between the theories. It has nothing to say about the truth or falsity of the various theories. Lichtheim correctly perceives that if he is to retain a notion of false consciousness, he will have to have a clear idea of what con-stitutes 'true consciousness'. He never actually tells us what 'true consciousness' is, or how he recognizes it when he sees it, and how he knows it to be true. To be sure, this is asking rather a lot, but if the job cannot be done, is it not simply more honest to adopt a relativist position?

Another difficulty: if one uses the word 'ideology' to refer only to false consciousness, it is legitimate to bring writers into the dis-cussion who never used the word 'ideology'. Lichtheim, following closely the work of Hans Barth in *Wahrheit und Ideologie*, manages to bring Hegel and Nietzsche into his discussion, though they did not use the word.[19] The worrying thing about this pro-cedure is that it is too strong. If ideology is 'about' the distortion of reality in thought, a history of the matter ought to include much more. Why not include Plato? Aristotle? Augustine? Thomas? The point here is that this way of using the term is too inclusive to be of much use.

But a more serious difficulty arises over the logical necessity to define a notion of truth and urge that this truth is the special property of social groups. This objection is advanced by Nigel Harris, a political Marxist.[20] Harris's critique (on this point) goes little beyond Mannheim; what is of interest is his inclusion of a relativist concept within the context of the Marxist general posi-tion 'I hold freedom to be the most important single ideal . . . I do identify freedom with the historical aims of the industrial working classes of the developed countries'.[21]

Precisely because 'our reality is the next man's ideology and vice-versa', Harris is suspicious of the supposed contrast between ideology (distorted, false view of reality) and a true view.[22] His sharpest barbs on this point are reserved, reasonably enough, for Parsons. Parsons is quoted as saying: 'The criterion of distortion is that statements are made about society which, by social science methods, can be shown to be positively in error.' Harris remarks: 'Thus "reality" here means what social scientists . . . say it is, and ideology is ideological in so far as it diverges from the account of reality offered by social scientists.'[23] The same applies to philosophical Marxists.

Harris proposes that what he calls 'practical tests' rather than 'logical disproof' are the appropriate tests for an ideology. The interesting thing about an ideology, that is to say, is whether or not it leads the group which accepts it to achieve their goals. The question of whether or not the statements which comprise an ideology are accurate or even sensible is a secondary matter. If, for example, a proletarian ideology contains a myth about (I use Sorel's example) the overwhelming power of a general strike, the important thing about this myth is whether it encourages the workers to actions which benefit them. That the 'myth' is more an aspiration than a realistic notion when it is formulated and propagated is a secondary matter.

Statements such as these may strike us as being a bit Machiavellian. Perhaps they are none the worse for that. For surely Machiavelli's point is that the ruler must accept responsibility for the success or failure of his ventures. The underlying belief is that social action involves concerted action by many men. Practical Marxists, those actually engaged in trying to create a revolution, men such as Lenin and Gramsci, have acknowledged this truth.[24] The nice counterpoint between truth and falsity which so exercises philosophical Marxists disappears from the political perspective. It is only fair, however, to point out that this does not mean that there is no such contrast, nor that it cannot be delineated. Such delineation is, indeed, the proper business of philosophers and scientists. It is merely to argue that it is unrealistic to expect such distinctions to be manifested in the differences between widely held and acted-on beliefs. And if pedigrees for such statements are called for, *that* realism is as much *Platonic* (the philosopher back in the cave; noble lies) as Machiavellian.

That said, there is at least one widespread political disposition for which a notion of false consciousness remains crucial. I have in mind the point of view which I associate with such figures as Herbert Marcuse and the Fabians, and which I can only characterize as paternalist. The paternalist believes that he knows what ends and means are really in the interests of other men (typically those less formally educated). It may also be held that it is good for people to live austerely, and that a government which restricts the supply of sweets when there are abundant supplies, or which insists on making publicly owned housing estates as drab and uniform as possible, is doing its proper job. The point about a paternalist is that he knows well that people do not, by and large, *want* to live in this way. He expects disagreement between his notions and those of his 'children'; he may even welcome it. He denies that people, on the average, ought to get what they want by saying that they are falsely conscious. This disposition owes much to philosophical Marxism's ideas about ideology. Marcuse adds one sophistication to the argument by adding that people do not really want what they say they want. They have been misled by advertising and other forms of ideology into desiring things they might not otherwise want. Despite the moralist flavour of this use of ideology, I cannot suppress a bias against it in favour of Lenin's position. Gramsci's followers always have the safeguard against him that he must carry them with him to a large extent or lose all authority; the paternalists brook no such political interference in their work.

## V

Political Marxists, like Harris, Deutscher, Lenin and Gramsci, have little use for the notion of ideology as false consciousness. They emphasize the role of ideas in the class struggle. Society is a struggle, in their view, between opposed classes. Ideas are weapons in this struggle. All ideas about society are weapons in this struggle. In so far as they can be marshalled into arguments and programmes, these ideas are what political Marxists call ideologies.

Marx realized that the workers suffered a number of disadvantages in this struggle. By and large, they lacked any genuine consciousness of themselves as a class; their enemy, the bourgeois, has recently learned the lessons of their common interest as a class. Thus the enemy is prepared; he has already equipped himself with an ideology while the proletariat have none. Moreover, since the bourgeois have come to power, they have nothing further to gain from class struggles; thus it is in their interest to believe that struggle, even class, does not exist. The proletariat have therefore to combat at once the attacks upon them in the bourgeois ideology and the ideological idea that class struggle is a thing of the past.

Alasdair MacIntyre's recent attacks on what he calls the 'end of ideology ideology' are a revived form of this argument.[25]

Thus one of the main tenets of proletarian thought, as the political Marxist sees it, must be the notion that supposedly class-neutral social and moral theories are part of the bourgeois ideology. Here we see the full impact of the view that all ideas are part of one or other ideology. Ideas are measured by their consequences in the class struggle (their 'objective truth', as it is sometimes put), and never by the intention of their authors.

The impact of this view is sharpened when we take into account the further Marxist notion that the class struggle can be won by the workers only in some kind of revolutionary cataclysm. This last notion means that attempts to improve the actual living conditions of the workers are looked upon with considerable misgiving. If such attempts 'buy off' the workers, they make the task of creating a revolutionary class consciousness the more difficult. It matters not where these ideas originate: Lenin was much concerned by the development of a 'trade union' consciousness. From his point of view, this is understandable enough: if the postal workers strike for higher wages and receive no support from the miners who again receive no support from the engineering workers, then the workers are acting as members of unions, not as members of a class.

It is when one compares this point of view with that of the philosophically inclined Marxists that one comes to appreciate the dispute between Lichtheim and Lenin over the notion of a 'Marxist ideology'. From the perspective of the political Marxists, the ideas of the various classes are on a par. They attack each other. Thus it seems hardly objectionable to refer to one's own ideology as well as that of the enemy. This would not be the first time that practising politicians have adopted and used themselves unflattering descriptions originally used to condemn. The terms 'Whig' and 'Tory' are two examples of unflattering descriptions now accepted by those against whom they were originally aimed; the Democratic and Republican Parties, too, adopt the unflattering cartoonist's symbols, the donkey and the elephant. Might it be that in the relative heat of real battle the economy of symbolic expression which each of these terms gives is taken to outweigh the disadvantages which so upset others? Be this as it may, it is interesting to observe that Marxism contains a school which does not flinch from referring to its own ideology where neither Liberals nor Conservatives have such a school. It is certainly worth considering that this feature of Marxism flows from the fact that it – unlike the other theories we shall be considering – has a practical wing. Liberalism and Conservatism are academic ideologies in a way which Marxism is not.

Notoriously deviant branches of Marxism are condemned as part of the bourgeois ideology. This is one obvious effect of the use of the notion of ideology to refer to the effects of writings. There is a severity about this doctrine which contracts vividly with the, at times almost sloppy, tolerance of Liberalism. For political Marxists, as Lenin insisted in the passage quoted above (p. 163), there is no third way; either you are with us or not. But there is also one less obvious, if equally important, effect of this notion; it allows the inclusion on one's side of one's enemy's enemies. Marx speaks warmly of Aristotle and Shakespeare and their ethical ideas. The reason for this is that these pre-bourgeois writers attacked ideas which had become bourgeois virtues. Both Aristotle and Shakespeare can be cited against the practice of capital accumulation for its own sake. They are thus an ally against a common foe. Ironically, then, Social Democracy is part of the bourgeois ideology where Aristotle's notion of a 'political man' is taken to be a healthy ideal type.

In some form or other, political Marxism has become the dominant radical force in Western European politics. In so becoming, it has replaced the indigenous radical political movements in the various Western countries. In Europe, and very recently in America, this replacement of an older radicalism has meant a move from a Liberal concern with symbolic achievement (universal suffrage, most noticeably) to a concern with material goods. This movement seems to me to make good political sense – more people are likely to want things rather than symbols – but it is justified on grounds of a movement from mere politics to fundamental things. Perhaps such a move was on the cards in any case, perhaps the older Radicalism was a spent force, and certainly some of its most popular figures like Tom Paine were interested, if in an unsympathetic way, in a redistribution of wealth.

Perhaps, too, Marxism owes something of its success to the very real similarity between its values and those of the Victorian world it was attacking. Some of the great Liberal achievements and

strategies are translated by Marx into possible proletarian achievements. The notion of class solidarity is manifestly borrowed from
bourgeois experience. The argument is tacitly from analogy; the
bourgeois overthrew the aristocracy when they learned to act as a
class, so the proletariat ought to do the same. Similarly, the notion
that a proletarian–bourgeois struggle must benefit the ascendant
class just as the bourgeois–aristocratic struggle benefited its
ascendant class is based entirely on the logic of analogy. There
cannot, in principle, be a historical argument because the proletariat were not yet class-conscious. This is not to deride Marxism,
and it is certainly not to say that it is wrong –there are times, and
predicting future events is one of them, when analogy is inescapable; but the point is that Marxists impose (*must* impose) notions
taken from outside working-class experience if they are to lead
that class to something entirely new to it.

It might be objected that revolutionary class consciousness
seems even further from realization today than when Marx wrote.
This is surely a disappointment for Marxists, hardly much more.
Those determined to believe that the revolution is coming will not
so easily be dissuaded. A more fundamental difficulty arises over
the notion that we all ought to be 'political men' of the Aristotelian
ideal type. This notion is obviously not derived from Victorian
experience; it was not a typical bourgeois ideal type. In positing it
as his goal, Marx goes well beyond bourgeois experience.

At this point, political Marxism stands in need of help from the
philosophers. Philosophical Marxism tells us that the new man
will have overcome the characteristic deficiencies of bourgeois
society. He will no longer be avaricious; he will no longer be
robbed of the real value of his work; he will no longer think in
ideological terms; he will no longer see himself as merely the
owner of his property; in other words, he will be free. Aside from
the matter that his freedom is rather negative – we are told much
about what it will *not* be like – is the question of how these middle-
class men know this is a true picture. The answer is that they have
already freed themselves from slavery to bourgeois ideology. They
know what the free life is, and after the revolution they will be
able to live that life. But surely that is a symbolic achievement if
ever there was one.

# 10 Conservatism

## I

We are in some danger of forgetting that there are two quite different Conservative traditions. For want of generally accepted names, I will call them 'Continental bureaucratic' and 'Anglo-Saxon sceptical' Conservatism. We, in English-speaking countries, are in danger of forgetting that there is such a distinction to be made because we have, for all real purposes, lost sight of the Continental variety. More the pity, because this lost variety has much to offer which we ought to remember. In order partly to keep the memory alive, but also in order to point to the inadequacies of our own variety of Conservatism, I mention it here.

The genius of Continental bureaucratic Conservatism, by which I mean the theory of politics which achieved its noblest expression in Hegel's *Philosophy of Right*, is its unflinching recognition of the key political fact of our time: bureaucracy. It is now something of a commonplace that all the major states of the world are similar in that most of the important political decisions in them are taken by, or at any rate prejudiced by, their bureaucracies.[1] But so far as ideologists are concerned, the chief function of this commonplace seems to be in mocking at Lenin. For all that trouble, we imply, the Soviets end up with a polity not so radically different from ours. This response by ideologists is simply not good enough. For if it is the case that an event so cataclysmic as the Russian Revolution results in little more than a change of personnel at the top, then ours is certainly an age of massive stability.

There are, of course, good reasons for thinking that this is the case. Then a large degree of bureaucratic control ought to be taken into account by our ideologies. This they patently do not do. The reasons why modern states must be bureaucratic were suggested by Hegel and adumbrated with a mass of detail by Weber.

One need only reflect on the chaos which could result if our governments were run by a prince and his secretary, as envisaged by Machiavelli, to see why a bureaucracy is needed. If the administration of, say, pensions were entrusted to one man, he could never remember all the rules, he would never be able to answer his correspondence, he would be hard put to recall precedent and would almost certainly not know what his predecessor did in any detail. And what would happen when he expired from overwork? What salary could compensate him sufficiently to protect him against the temptation to corruption? The very idea is grotesque. One need hardly elaborate the ramifications of doing without a bureaucracy. Individuals, no matter how excellent, cannot be depended on to carry out the complex tasks of a modern government unless organized into an administrative machine.

This is not said to celebrate the new dominance of the administrators, and certainly one can criticize Hegel and his school for being blind to the deficiencies of bureaucrats, but their role cannot be denied. But this is so obvious it should not need saying. It does need saying, however, and especially in a work on ideology. For none of our ideologies have come to grips with bureaucracy. None of them gives any serious thought to the problem, say, of citizen redress against maladministration – surely one of the most important problems of our day – and little enough thought to the problem of administrative recruitment.

This lack is deplorable enough in a professedly revolutionary ideology – though it is perhaps understandable and not unexpected; it is contemptible in an ideology which professes to conserve. To conserve, one ought at very least to know what is going on. Yet it is difficult to recall one sustained comment on these matters from English-speaking Conservatives since the Second World War. More usually one hears the automatic phrases of horror whenever bureaucracy is mentioned. One cannot help recalling a favourite refrain from Alben Barkley (Democratic vice-presidential candidate in 1948): 'What is a bureaucrat? A bureaucrat is a Democrat who has a job some Republican wants.' A bit unfair, perhaps, but precisely the kind of jibe this negative Conservative position is open to. British Conservatives seem largely concerned to prevent the world becoming what it has long since been.

Surely this is an exercise in unreality so thorough as to be sublime. The loss of reality is the greater for the fact that the essential features of bureaucracy were recognized and dealt with at length by Hegel and, following him, Weber. But the traditions which descend from them have never been integrated into the body of English Conservatism. One is entitled to wonder why.

One reason must surely be that English-speaking philosophy already contained a strong native Conservative school when Hegel arrived. What is more, the native school, in the subtle form given it by Hume as well as the more stirring form associated with Burke, was profoundly sceptical. Its fundamental belief was that men simply could not honestly claim to know what were the natural principles of right political action. This epistemological belief is reinforced by historical observation. The excesses which Continental peoples suffered during the Second World War are attributed to the indirect effects of politicians believing in abstract principles of right. Both these beliefs are general in British culture: Hobhouse, a Liberal, assigned German excesses in the First World War to Hegel; Conservatism combines them both and turns them into a point of view. How different is this cultural disposition from the Continental? The antagonism and incomprehension is mutual. In British eyes, nothing could be more strange and foreign than the abstract philosophizing of the Continental idealists.

Another reason why British Conservatives reject Continental influences is that these influences were felt first and thereafter associated with the Left. Hegel is associated in British eyes with Marx. He is the chap Marx stood on his head – not exactly a position to inspire respect. When Hegel's influence was felt in Britain, it was through Liberals such as T. H. Green and his school. When bureaucracy is considered seriously, it is in the works of the Fabians – again, not company for Tories. In general, opinion seems to be with R. H. S. Crossman when he says:

> Not till academic lectures had the good fortune to read Hegel could a philosophy be discovered obscure enough to justify [British institutions], and to persuade rational men that obedience to an irrational process of development was the supreme manifestation of reason. The British idealists, however, accomplished this task and in the works of Bradley, Green and Bosanquet an aura of philosophic profundity was cast around

the superstitious sanctifications of existing institutions and the 'law of their development'.

Apart from this aberration, which is fortunately past, British thinkers have been notoriously rationalist, free-thinking, and utilitarian.[2]

Scepticism about abstract theorizing, it seems, extends well beyond the officially recognized boundaries of the Tory Party.

## II

Scepticism seems not to have entered British political philosophy. It was always there. Looking for a source of this dominant strain is not likely to prove a useful enterprise. We must content ourselves with the knowledge that it has long been present. Bacon, Hobbes and Locke, system-builders though they subsequently became, began with scepticism. Bacon was sceptical about the authoritative doctrines of his day. He wanted to smash these idols and write a new logic. Hobbes (Bacon's secretary) was sceptical about the doctrines of the 'students of Aristotle'. He, none too modestly, saw himself as a wise man who used words for counters while fools accepted them as money. Locke, too, was touched by scepticism. In political matters he could not accept the claims of any regime to automatic obedience from its citizens; neither could he swallow the paternalist analogy upon which such claims were based in his time.

But none of these writers was a thoroughgoing sceptic. Each began with scepticism about the reasons and justifications being advanced by the intellectual and political authorities of their times. Each ended by replacing the fashionable doctrines with new ones – more secure justifications, or so they thought. Hume broke with this method. He argued that obedience to the law is (largely) a habit. Obedience is not (and cannot logically be) justified by any appeal to reason. It is not justified, for example, by some hypothetical or historical social contract. Neither is it justified by some affinity or approximation of the laws of the state to some Natural Law.

The laws of the state are merely conventions. They are not so much right as comfortable. The laws are rather like the language.

They can be, and are, changed in part from time to time. Indeed, there is hardly ever a time when some part or other of the law is not being changed. But change for its own sake, or too much change in all, is abhorrent; it confuses the dull wit of the citizenry, not to mention the Bench. Each specific new law can be readily understood and adapted to by the citizenry because it is seen to fit into the old well-worn fabric. The whole holds together and makes life tolerable, because predictable, because familiar. As it happens, such an arrangement is in the general interest. Civility and prosperity, not to mention justice, require a settled condition. But too much can be made of this fact. Very few people actually obey the law (in general or in specific cases) for this reason; we mostly lack the foresight.

Hume's scepticism extends to egoism. Men are not, on the whole, rational in the sense that they consistently and intelligently pursue their own selfish interests. And this is true as much of the governors as of the governed. There is no attempt here to justify government by an argument from the superior wisdom of the governors. We are all equally weak of mind and strong of passion; and yet, provided we do not meddle too much, there is no terrible price to be paid for this weakness. One is struck, and deeply attracted, by the gentleness of Hume's doctrines. He demands so little and forgives so much. Things work, society prospers despite our abundant clumsiness. If only the meddlesome doctrinaires do not ruin the stability of life, life will be tolerable enough.

How pleasant life would be if only one could accept that this was a satisfactory basis for a political philosophy; how much preferable Hume's view is to the earnest, strident priggishness of those who urge us to participate in politics incessantly. But there are more than a few trifling difficulties. To mention the most obvious, it is far from clear that life is tolerable enough for most people. To mention another, which ought to be more compelling to Conservatives, this gentle view affords no guide to the statesman. Some action or other must be taken in times of trouble. No statesman would retain the respect of even his closest aides if he did nothing whatever during a crisis. We expect some guide, or even a hint, from a political philosophy as to what kinds of thing the ruler ought to keep in mind. Nothing of the sort is forthcoming from Hume. Another difficulty, a less practical one, but logically important nonetheless, is that this gentle view proves too much.

It excludes nothing. If this society's laws are merely conventional, then so are every other's. There is nothing to choose between them. This kind of Conservatism can mock Jacobins and Bolsheviks for trying to change society radically, but that is about all it can do. It is against Lenin in October, but in November he is seen to be just another Russian autocrat. If that is all there is to be said in criticism of revolutionaries, we might all just as well join the cadres; after all, they know what they want.

When it comes to mocking Jacobins, however, one moves from the gentle conventionalism of Hume to Burke. Hume was a Scot, Burke an Irishman; Hume a bachelor, Burke a family man with numerous dependent relatives to support. Hume was the son of a minor landowner who rose at a very early age, by sheer brilliance of intellect, to dominate a backward, parochial, superstitious Edinburgh literary society. Burke fought for every advantage. His main talent was his rhetoric. He rose slowly and against strong prejudice in the sometimes wider world of London, by selling his pen to the highest bidder. Hume could defend what he knew from the inside and mock the doctrines of those he disliked. Burke's Conservatism was never entirely free of the taint of sycophancy. He was defending, near its end, the rule of a class he wanted too earnestly to join. He idealized manners he didn't have.

Burke idealized the past. He made a cult of tradition. The French Revolution, especially its Jacobin excesses, was the occasion of his greatest polemic, *Reflections on the Revolution in France*. 'Reflections' pitches the matter rather high. Burke's reaction approached panic. It caused him to break with his closest (Whig) political allies. It also brought forth his best polemics and marks unquestionably the birth of a self-conscious Conservatism.

Conservatism, as it developed in the train of Burke's polemic, has two faces: in the first place, it makes a cult of the past; in the second, it makes an enemy of all principled politics. As it happens, the actual content of the tradition which they defend is not very important to the Conservative argument. The argument fastens on the advantages, the comforts, of traditional life as such; only secondarily does it depend on the specific character of the tradition. The traditional form of government which the Jacobins destroyed was monarchical, so Burke turned reverently to the Bourbon. If he had witnessed Louis XIV's centralization of power, he would have decried monarchical centralization and praised the virtues of independent provinces.

Thus it is mildly amusing, but actually beside the point, that – as many of his critics have noted – Burke was none too careful about matters of historical detail. He praises the none too obvious virtues of the French queen extravagantly, but such historical considerations do not really touch him. The point is not that this tradition is divine, but that tradition *per se* is sacred. Thus Conservatives may, following Burke, defend this or that institution from time to time; here monarchy, there property-owning democracy, here an established religion, there an ancient constitution. This Conservatism is so purely formal – it argues in favour of conserving whatever there is to conserve – that it is without boundary. In order to avoid the threat of one doctrine and one revolution, we get a defence useful to every established tyranny.

There is, for all this, one element of British and American politics which has remained particularly sacred to Conservatism: the rule of law. The law, the common law of England and the United States, is not based on any underlying principle. It is not rational in the way Roman and Soviet law is meant to be. For this reason, and because the rule of law has remained such an important part of Anglo-American politics, this kind of sceptical Conservatism provides a particularly appropriate defence of this tradition. Anglo-American law embodies, so the Conservative theory goes, the decisions of generations of lawmakers, citizens, judges and police. It is the embodiment of the reason of the ages – that and nothing more. As such, it is collectively taken to be far wiser than any doctrine, no matter how popular, could ever be. Consequently any revolutionary doctrine is necessarily inadequate – and mistaken when it opposes the law as a whole. The wisdom (if that is what it is) of one generation could never be greater than that of all the past generations who have lived with and formed the common law. Life within the bounds of this law is civil – in both senses.

As this notion has come down to the end of the twentieth century, its most eloquent spokesman has been Michael Oakeshott.[3] Oakeshott claims that Conservatism is not a doctrine among other doctrines. It is simply not comparable with Liberalism and Socialism. On the contrary, Conservatism is a disposition:

. . . it is a disposition appropriate to a man who is acutely aware of having something to lose which he has learned to care for; a man in some degree rich in opportunities for enjoyment, but not so rich that he can afford to be indifferent to less.[4]

This disposition leads Conservatives to identify ideology as their prime enemy in the contemporary world. This is the second face of Burke and Conservatism. Scepticism about the reality of social theory leads to a condemnation of principled politics as such.

### III

The fullest elaboration of Oakeshott's views on the state of politics occurs in his essay 'Rationalism in Politics'. His most explicit statements about ideology occur in 'Political Education'.[5] The former essay was published in 1947, the latter in 1951. The dates are of some interest. Britain was then ruled by a Labour government and, as the introduction of the second essay makes clear, Harold Laski (Oakeshott's immediate predecessor at the L.S.E.) is the ideologist he criticizes. Absurd though the notion now seems, Oakeshott obviously believed he had followed a British Marx (or perhaps a Trotsky) into his chair. The point of his critique is to save Britain from the fate of Russia and Germany, from the excesses and rigidity of ideology. In place of Marx and Lenin, he saw himself faced with Harold Laski and Clem Attlee.[6]

This idea would be difficult to take seriously were it less common. Much of the reaction against ideology can be seen, in its historical context, to be a reaction against 'totalitarianism'. The Liberal form of that reaction will be examined in the next chapter. Here we are concerned with the Conservative form of that reaction. Sometimes, as in Talmon's *The Origins of Totalitarian Democracy* (1952) and Friedrich and Brzezinski's *Totalitarian Dictatorship and Autocracy* (1956), a distinction is made between ideology as such and totalitarian ideology.[7] But the distinction is of little historical or theoretical interest. The main theme of this literature is that all ideologies, all attempts to create 'action-related' systems of ideas, necessarily become totalitarian. Friedrich and Brzezinski say:

When theory is applied to a real-life situation, there are usually two alternatives : one is to modify the theory so as to make it more compatible with the prerequisites of practice, and the other is to attempt to force history to fit their conception of it. And when such a conception involves a far-reaching idea of the desirable, that is historically inevitable, scheme of social organisation, the efforts to mould society to fit it, and the consequent measures to break down the resistance to it, result in totalitarianism.[8]

The subject of these abstract remarks is specific enough: Soviet Marxism and German and Italian Fascism. The subject is thus the same as in the Liberal critique of ideology. What is different is the reasons given for fearing the ideologies.

For Liberals, the reason is the ideologists' intolerance. For Conservatives it is their rigidity and comprehensiveness. The Conservative comes to grips with the horrors of the concentration camps and the frightening willingness with which otherwise civilized Germans and Russians allowed themselves to be welded into the unified tool of their leaders by blaming it all on a previous rejection of Conservative practice.[9]

Hannah Arendt, to cite another example, contrasts the rule of ideology with the rule of law.[10] She emphasizes the moderating influences of a rule of law. She claims that in a polity governed by law, the government cannot have total power over the citizens: the citizen is protected from the arbitrary exercise of power. This is good classical stuff; it echoes of Aristotle and Montesquieu. Perhaps it was true of the law as they knew it, but can anyone really maintain that it is true of the law in, say, present-day Chicago?

Arendt thinks that, in a totalitarian country, by way of contrast, the safest place for a man to be is under arrest. In that condition at least one cannot be accused of new crimes. This strikes me as no comfort at all: how safe was Rubashov?

Ideologies teach, she believes, the replacement of the positive laws of the state by the ruthless laws of historical inevitability. Against such a law there is no redress. This way lies tyranny: 'The truth is, rather, that the real nature of all ideologies was revealed only in the role that the ideology plays in the apparatus of totalitarian domination.'[11] It seems that the road to Dachau is paved with bad ideas.

These Conservative critiques of ideology, originally inspired by the events surrounding the Second World War, have been revived more recently. The brief rise of the New Left in the late 1960s, the American anti-Vietnam war movement, the uprising of French students and workers in 1968, and the feeble echoes of these risings in British universities, have revived the Conservative anti-ideology.[12] Cohn-Bendit and Marcuse, the prophets of these brief risings, called for a total revolution. Society was to be made anew on the basis of a new system of values possessed by the young and the disenfranchised. The prophecies were answered in the now familiar Conservative form. Several of the contributors to Maurice Cranston's *The New Left* emphasize the rigidity of their opponents' ideas. R. A. Dahl's *After the Revolution* makes the point. As the symptoms of the disease recur, so the old medicines are brought out.

But what is the source, the original intellectual error which started Western man down this road? This is one of the subjects of contention among the Conservative anti-ideologists. They do agree, however, that the source is deep in the intellectual past. Leo Strauss points an accusing finger at Hobbes (or was it Machiavelli?) – in any case at historicism and the break from the belief in Natural Law.[13] Eric Voeglin points to Gnosticism, to secular politics, and suggests that Richard Hooker, author of *Ecclesiastical Polity* (1594), was the first to spot the trend. Talmon points to Helvétius and Holbach; Arendt to anti-Semitism. Ideological original sin occurred long ago.

This fact – the belief that somehow Dachau is traceable to some sixteenth- or seventeenth-century error which has come to pervade political thinking – points to how utterly pessimistic and unhelpful this kind of Conservatism is. If everything said since, say, Hobbes is wrong, if every major change of course since the seventeenth century is a step into totalitarianism, we might as well learn to love it. Even if one leaves aside for the moment the argument that political theory in the modern world is not entirely capricious, that it in some sense fits the world it accompanies, there is surely no aspect of the general stock of ideas about politics which survives this period in unaltered form. All the ideas we have – not least Conservatism – are products of post-Hobbesian thinking. It is possible, of course, that some future thinker will revive Aristotelian political science; in some ways it is an attractive prospect. But such a revival would have to begin by dropping much of the Aristotelian teaching; it would be a new, modern system which emerged. This is surely the Conservative dilemma: the present is condemned as inherently ideological, the only alternative is something radically new, but could any new theory be Conservative?

## IV

Two problems for these Conservatives emerge at this point: firstly, what is it about ideological thinking which has led it away from Conservative practice; and secondly, what does a healthy political polity look like? We need answers to these questions in order to bring Conservatism into focus, in order to see what kind of world it wants and how it proposes to get there. I take it as given that any remotely adequate political theory must answer these questions. Without some notion of what kind of world is desired by Conservatives, we should never really understand what they dislike about the present situation – and there can be little doubt that, of all the ideologies discussed here, Conservatism is, ironically, the least comfortable in the modern world; without some idea of how they propose to relieve us of the errors of modernity, we should not know how (if at all) serious they are.

Taken strictly, Conservatives would deny that they have a picture of an ideal political world. Such pictures strike them as suspiciously ideological. All the same, there is a deeper level at which they do have an ideal, and this ideal gives them a model against which to hold the present ideology-intoxicated world.

Oakeshott, to return to their most sublime spokesman, has an image of a completely unreflective, unselfconscious traditional polity. As opposed to the ideological style of politics, there is the traditional pursuit of intimations: 'In politics, every enterprise is a consequential enterprise, the pursuit, not of a dream, or of a general principle, but an intimation.[14] The image is impacted into one stunningly obscure phrase: 'the pursuit of intimations'. What, one must ask, is an intimation? He later added, in response to criticism on just this point, that his expression 'is neither intended as a description of the motives of politicians, nor of what they believe themselves to be doing'.[15] This addition merely serves to rule out the only reasonable interpretations one can give to the phrase.

This is something of a tragedy for Conservatism; for surely it is the case that politicians' decisions can often be described as acting on hunch, or as based on their feel for what the situation at hand demands. Moreover, acting in this way rather than in response to the logic of some ideology or according to the cunning of some selfish reason is close to the essence of responsible political action. Oakeshott's addition successfully turns his philosophy away from the salient wisdom of Conservatism. The notion, too easily parodied for anyone's good, that Conservatives place their faith in men, not measures, is not to be dismissed. Politics is in large part an art which requires the skill of a practised man, just like any other art. Such a man will always be superior to the ideologue; to the man who does not bother to take the feeling of opinion before acting, who is so certain he is right that he has no patience for other mortals. If this is not what is meant by 'pursuing intimations', what is?

One can judge this best by looking at the reasons given for avoiding the major alternative style – the ideological. Oakeshott says that an ideology is an abridgement of a tradition. So, in part, it is. Ideologies like Marxism depend very heavily for their rhetorical pull upon an abridgement of the working-class myths about capitalism. Sorel makes a similar point, though to different ends. But there are other elements in Marxism. It contains a heavy dose of Hegelian logic and Scottish economic theory, for example, which are left out of Oakeshott's characterization in such a way as to make his position something of an abridgement itself.

Acting on an abridgement of a tradition is only to be faulted if it is possible to do better: to act on complete knowledge. Oakeshott believes this a real choice: '[this] suggests that a knowledge of the chosen political ideology can take the place of understanding a tradition of political behaviour'.[16] It is assumed that there are (or were), somewhere in the world, a people who actually 'understood a tradition' and who acted on the intimations which flow from this knowledge. Do such people exist?

Given the admitted ideological intoxication of contemporary Western civilization, we must look for such a traditional people elsewhere. We might expect to find them in other civilizations, or in our own past. At first glance, the first alternative sounds promising. After all, does not a large body of anthropological research point to the existence of pre-rational traditional societies? Does not the distinction between traditional and legal-rational domination occur in Weber and, in nascent form, in Hegel?

The distinction does occur in Weber. It constitutes two parts of his famous threefold classification of patterns of dominance: charismatic, traditional and legal-rational. Fascinating and influential though this classification is, our present purpose will be served by noting that (a) the distinction is historical (the traditional mode is in our past); (b) the traditional mode may well survive in other parts of the world but was superseded in the West by the rise to the modern state. This much is in harmony with the Conservative distinction between an ideological and a traditional society, even if the emphasis is different.

Comfort for Conservatives may be derived, too, from the anthropological research which Weber is, in part, responsible for having inspired. But more recent research tends to play down the distinction: to suggest that self-conscious manipulation of the traditional and creation of self-serving abridgements of tradition characterizes 'traditional' non-Western societies in a familiar way. One example from a 'traditional' society proves little, but it does illustrate a successful manipulation of tradition so patently human as to throw doubt on the notion that there is any other way of doing things.

My example comes from a paper by Leopold Pospisil. Pospisil argues that a multiplicity of legal systems (he used 'legal' in a broad way to characterize any system of rules; he is willing to talk of the legal system of a family) are found in every society. These systems can, and in a relatively small society often do, conflict. The inhabitants of such a society may be aware of the potential conflicts, and will, given the opportunity, play one off against the other to suit temporary advantage, using any excuse – such as an abridgement of one system of law – which comes to mind. He cites the example of

... Awiitigaaji, the headman of the village of Botukebo. ... This man fell in love with his beautiful third cousin who, unfortunately, belonged to the same sib as he. Kapauku law is very explicit about the matter of incest. It categorically states: ... 'to marry one's sibmate is taboo'. Nevertheless, Awiitigaaji did not hesitate to break the taboo and he eloped with the girl. The infuriated relatives of the couple pursued the lovers, and the girl's father, the late Ugataga, who held the position of head-man in the neighbouring village of Kojogeepa, ruled that both his daughter and Awiitigaaji must be punished according to the Kapauku customary law by being shot to death. The dangerous situation was accepted by the fugitive Awiitigaaji, who was well versed in native law and intrigue, as a challenge. Through his understanding of the problem and through skilful political moves and clever manipulation of his relatives, he succeeded not only in going unpunished, but also in keeping the girl as wife.[17]

This example is adduced here to foreclose a possible argument for a traditional political practice different from our own. It is only fair to add, however, that the Conservatives whose ideas about ideology I have been considering have not sought to appeal to anthropological evidence. They are concerned with that other possible place of a traditional politics: the Western past.

In this they are on even weaker ground. Oakeshott, in par-ticular, abridges the events of the pre-rationalist world into an ideology of 'tradition' which is, in many ways, even more fanciful than the ideologies of 'natural rights' and 'justice' which he de-plores. His abridgement of Western life before the fourteenth and fifteenth centuries is of a world in which the opportunity for choice was narrowly circumscribed:

> To know oneself as a member of a family, a group, a corpora-tion, a church, a village community, as a suitor at a court or as the occupier of a tenancy, has been for the vast majority the circumstantially possible sum of self-knowledge. Not only were ordinary activities, those concerned with getting a living, com-munal in character, but so also were decisions, rights and responsibilities. Relationships and allegiances normally sprang from status and rarely extricated themselves from the analogy of kinship. For the most part anonymity prevailed; individual human character was rarely observed because it was not there to be observed. What differentiated one man from another was insignificant when compared with what was enjoyed in common as members of a group of some sort.[18]

This is the world we are thought to have lost. It is a pleasant picture, but a picture and, for all that, a radical abridgement of a world lost. It is a picture which has attracted people from the other end of the political spectrum as much as Conservatives. One of its great advantages is that it is set in a period so deeply lost to us by the scarcity of reliable historical documents that it is not likely to be disturbed.

In its way there is nothing particularly pernicious about this kind of image. It is no less worth admiring than a Biblical promise of an imaginary commonwealth. And yet there is something uneasy about this kind of abridgement. A Conservatism which has to turn this far back into the past to find a world in which it can imagine itself comfortable, which must disown everything which has happened since, is a Conservatism full of self-hatred.

This theory bespeaks a failure of confidence of frightening proportions.

# 11 Liberalism

## I

As there are several kinds of Conservatism, so there are several kinds of Liberalism. It may help us to keep them straight if we relate them through the authors who put their case most cogently.

Firstly, there is classical Liberalism, the political philosophy of seventeenth- and eighteenth-century radicals. This is the philosophy whose locus is to be found in the writings of John Locke. This doctrine portrays men as modest characters of moderate passions and feeble reason. They can best be accommodated to one another by government which interferes with them as little as possible. From 'feeble reason' a theorist can argue for strong government (as Hobbes did) from the need to protect the weakling; or for weak government (as anarchists do) from fear of the weakness of the governor's reason. Classical Liberalism takes the latter path – and thus, by the way, paves the way for anarchism, which is only an extreme form of this theory – putting its faith in the self-controlling mechanisms. 'The market' is the most important of these mechanisms. In it each individual sells his labour to the highest bidder and buys his goods from the cheapest seller. Since the market is much too complex for any one person, or group of people, to control, all the important economic decisions affecting a man are made without conscious policy on the part of anyone. The genius of such a scheme is that no doctrine – such as the notion of a just price – is necessary to its operation and hence there is no need for any government to interfere in these matters. The operation of the mechanism of the market is thus supposed to eliminate the need for most governmental actions.

A key emphasis of this kind of Liberalism is placed on the 'right to property'. A moderate amount of property is said to give its owner freedom from economic domination, a sense of responsibility which springs from his need to husband his resources, and just enough work to do to keep his mind off troublesome revolutions and intrigues. 'Property' in this theory is generally taken to be land. After the fortuitous discovery of North America with its abundant natural wealth and sparse population, it was just about possible to believe that every man could reasonably expect to have a sufficient amount of property.

By the middle of the nineteenth century it was evident that this picture, no matter how attractive, would not do in an industrial world. The concentration of wealth and the resultant pauperization of the masses on the one hand, and the immense power of a united proletariat on the other, makes it clear that something additional remains to be said. Of course, the proletariat were rarely enough united, but the memory of the French Revolution – and later 1848 and 1871 – cast long shadows. There were two responses to the new situation: rejection of the entire scheme, Marx's action, or its revision as with J. S. Mill. Mill's work marks the turning-point between classical Liberalism and contemporary Liberalism.

Marx did not find the classical Liberal picture very attractive. To him it was part of the bourgeois ideology. It expressed the bourgeois fear of a strong central government which, at this stage in history, it did not control. It also provided a convenient moral justification for early capitalists' desires to move their money to the most likely lucrative use without government restraint. On Marx's view, this kind of Liberalism had an important historical role to play – it led the bourgeois to power and to the smashing of feudalism and mercantalism – but it had become a reactionary ideology. It came to serve to justify the government's efforts to prevent the creation of a strong working-class movement. Moreover, the picture of individual men peaceably pursuing their own interests without interference from government was a ruse. Men, on Marx's view, are more than possessive individualists. They would really be much happier – and much more human – if incessant labour were not needed from all, and if each could enjoy a little fishing and perhaps some reading in the evening.

Mill was not strongly opposed to the doctrines of his fathers. Neither was he prepared to resort to Marx's extreme remedies. Even less was he convinced that all real social danger came from the side of the wealthy few. An equal danger was to be found in the combined weight of the vulgar many. Liberty for all required that neither the few nor the many dominate completely but that each have its due. This could be accomplished only if all points of view could be heard in public. Tolerance of all views, the freedom of speech, must be guaranteed so that, in a marketplace for ideas, the most rational would be accepted by all. This tolerance, and the rational acceptance of argument which is supposed to flow from it, is meant, among other things, to ensure that the powerful – be they the wealthy or the vulgar – do not convince by dint of their power alone.

The Liberalism which concerns us is a direct descendant of Mill's revision of classical Liberalism. Its tenets are readily enough listed: tolerance is its chief social virtue; it believes that a decent life for all is best protected in a society in which every interest is allowed expression and access to power; it believes safety lies in the existence of a large number of such groups; it believes that the current British and American regimes exemplify such virtues.

As with Conservatism, one of the most revealing things about Liberalism is what it leaves out of account. Contemporary Liberalism is innocent of any coherent economic doctrine. It has thrown off its heritage of *laissez-faire* economic doctrines. It nowhere agrees with J. S. Mill about a government's right to sort out patterns of distribution to favour the poor. Marxist criticisms of classical Liberalism have, in effect, been accepted. It says nothing whatever about wealth, its distribution, or the correct policy of governments to wealth.

Historically, this fastidiousness is the result of having theoretical fingers burnt on the subject of the poor. Classical Liberalism was not conceived of by its proponents as a class doctrine. It was not meant to be a tool for the rich to beat the poor with. When it became obvious that this was the way in which it was being used, a tactical retreat was called. Our Liberals would avoid the attacks which Locke's notion of the right to property attracted by silence on the question of wealth altogether.

In one way, however, this retreat can be turned to advantage by Liberals. They can claim that the pro-capitalist bias of Locke's work was not essential to it. The essential point was to guard the rights of individuals against other individuals and against the state. If changed historical conditions reveal an unintended bias, this bias was not essential anyhow. It can be dropped.

The new purified doctrine seeks to be neutral between the proponents of capitalism and those of Socialism. On a political level, they seek to be neutral between capital and organized labour. And this, I think, gives us an important clue to Liberalism. It replaces the classical Liberal notion of a society of free, equal, competing individuals with a notion of free, substantially equal and ferociously competing interest groups.

'Pluralism' is the name we give to this doctrine when it clothes itself in the robes of political science. The name accurately reflects its practitioners' beliefs that theirs is a world in which all is for the best, since the plurality of interest groups is tolerated on an equal footing and each is allowed to fight for its goals. Firemen, bakers, Indian chiefs are all given a chance – an equal chance. The most clear-cut, if also the most benign statements of this view can be found in David B. Truman's *The Governmental Process*.[1]

This doctrine, whether one calls it Liberalism or Pluralism, must be innocent of any idea of economic rationality for the reason that it seeks to be neutral on this ground. Since money is the thing most political arguments are about – certainly the thing most political arguments in our world are about – Liberalism will avoid taking sides on the question. It will be above the fray since it believes that safety – and it is very concerned with safety – rests in the balance between the competing groups, not in the rightness of one group's cause.

This is a most singular doctrine. The most important subject of political argument is – **because** it is the most important subject of political discussion – bracketed out of theoretical discussion. Let us assume for the moment that it is an accurate view. Let us accept, with Liberals, that the safety of the individual from the arbitrary action of governments or private interests is the most important goal of social action. Let us allow that this safety is achieved best by letting the various interest groups have it out in an unrestrained battle in the political arena. Let us allow that this political free-for-all will actually protect the individual – largely because the various groups will be competing for his support or the support of his representative to the extent that they wouldn't dare trample on him. Given all this, will this kind of Liberalism do? Hardly.

It will not do, primarily because it is based firmly, if implicitly, on an incoherent notion of human nature. 'Man', the individual who is meant to be protected by this free competition between interest groups, is the product of a kind of 'double-bind'. On the one hand, this man is honoured and protected as he is a competitive acquisitive creature, and yet on the other he is punished – by the withdrawal of praise – when his effort is successful. What other interpretation is one to give to a theory which requires all men to compete for resources – and makes it quite clear that this is the only serious way for a man to spend his time – to form alliances of like-minded men to compete against other groups, and who is castigated if he is successful? For is it not the case that Liberals blame most ferociously those who succeed too well?

In America during the 1930s, Liberalism was the ally of disorganized labour. Now that labour is well enough organized to throw its weight around, Liberals abandon it. Now it is discovered to be in secret league with oligarchic capital against the consumer and the unemployed. So it is, of course, but is there not something missing in a doctrine which did not lead one to expect such action? Against this squeamish distaste for power – could there be a worse attitude from which to reflect on politics – one cannot help but prefer the consistent ruthlessness of a Tory or a Communist.

One is struck by the power of the analogy between this Liberal attitude to wealth and power and some of the practices on Israeli kibbutzim – surely itself the most ebullient child of Western Liberalism. Bruno Bettelheim describes the sexual education of kibbutz children.[2] Their parents, in a reaction against the puritanism of the ghettos from which they fled, put their children into communal housing arrangements in which boys and girls live until they (both) join the army.

The children are in a 'double-bind' and develop defensive attitudes to their own bodies – not wanting to be touched, for instance – because, on the one hand, they are taught to see their own and other children's bodies 'naturally' and they are yet exhorted to keep themselves 'pure'. Premarital pregnancy is heavily frowned on. The theory is that lust can be avoided by seeing sexual differences as 'natural' in everyday childhood life. The practice seems to be a repression of the sexual desire thus engendered. The kibbutz children are subject to an attitude to sex very like the attitude to wealth and power which underlies Liberalism. In both cases the theory predicates a human nature flawed by a 'lie in the soul'.

From a theoretical perspective, a flaw of this kind is conclusive. A political theory, no matter how accurately it portrays political activity, is unsatisfactory if it is based on an obnoxious notion of humanity. We demand that political theories depict – among other things – how we ought to construct the political kingdom on the basis of a realistic understanding of human experience. But some people always find such criticism unmoving. These people are not troubled by descriptions of human nature. On the contrary, they reject the greater part of political philosophy just because it is so concerned with human nature. They lower the standard against which a theory is tested. They wish to know (merely?) whether or not the theory accurately describes or explains actual political activity. How does Liberalism measure up on this standard?

## II

Let it be noted, in the first place, that this is the kind of criticism which contemporary Liberals must accept. When Karl Popper criticizes the closed society and its friends he is speaking out about how the Soviet Union is actually run. His contrast is with what he calls an open society, by which he means, first of all, the United States.[3] Raymond Aron contrasts 'constitutional-pluralist' regimes (France mainly, but also the United Kingdom) with monopolistic party regimes (the Soviet Union). Aron puts the point:

> Politically, what seems to me decisive is that in Western-type systems, one finds a plurality of organisations, independent of the state; in the Soviet regimes, enterprises or trusts do enjoy a certain measure of administrative or legal autonomy, but each organised group is, of necessity, linked to the state and conse-quently subordinated to its ideology.[4]

Bernard Crick, whose book *In Defence of Politics* is the best contemporary statement of the old Whig position, uses different terms – he contrasts the political regimes with the totalitarian regime – to the same effect as Popper and Aron.[5] Camus's *Rebel* belongs to the same literature, at least in the important sense that he contrasts totalitarian murder with trade union rebellion. All these Liberals are speaking about – and defending – the regimes of the West.[6]

F

This defence is based on a sociological notion – well adumbrated in Aron's work, merely alluded to by Popper and Camus – that power is diffused and individuals' interests protected in the West, because of the unrestricted actions of pressure groups. Trade unions are a favourite example of such a pressure group. The theory is that workers can, by banding together into unions, exert sufficient leverage against their employers and governments to see to the protection of members' interests. A crucial notion is that all men can join, or create, such groups and thus none are especially privileged or disadvantaged.

This last claim is crucial, for it serves to smuggle into the theory a notion that the system operates fairly. If this claim is sustained, then we have a theory which not only describes the inner workings of Western politics, but also serves to justify them. The early Liberal and radical notion that a government is legitimate if it is, as Lincoln summarized it, '*of*, *by* and *for* the people', is replaced. The earlier notion has to be replaced and, in effect, watered down if any contemporary government is to be legitimate, because no government today can even hope to make credible any notion that is *of* or *by* the people. The machinery is just too complex, the road to power too long and narrow. If most American boys still want to be President when they grow up, they soon learn better. Given these intractable political problems to democratic rule, a weaker justification is called for.

Liberals believe – and here, as with Conservatives, the events of the Second World War and the Cold War did much to sharpen the arguments – that politics in their countries is better than politics elsewhere. If the main democratic arguments for a country's legitimacy – the claim that its government is *of*, *by* and *for* the people – are rendered incredible, then a weaker defence will just have to do. Hence the importance of the notion that pluralism is a game all can play without disadvantage. Once this is admitted, the Liberal can still imply that his is a country in which the government, however remote, complex and incomprehensible it is, is at least a government *for* the people. It works in everyone's interest. Its being *for* the people – and this is the only justification offered for it – is said to result naturally from the way the public machine responds impartially to the pressure exerted on it by the various interest groups.

This theory requires the existence of a 'public ear' open to

argument from any group. The whole justification would break
down if even one group were denied a hearing. In such cases,
some people would be less equal than others; hence the superiority
of the Liberal societies to totalitarianism would be lost.

This is to say that any claim must be heard. Tolerance is the
keynote. But, and this is important to notice, it is not a merely
negative position; it is not merely a matter of ensuring that no one
is excluded from access to the 'public ear'. It is also a matter of
self-restraint on the part of the better-established, more powerful
groups. If the tolerant willingness to hear any group is to be
sustained, those groups who already have the public ear must
refrain from pouring any positive philosophy into it. Where tolerance is the key virtue, the public theory is merely formal. It does
not exclude anything. There can be no question of ruling certain
theories out of order because they are, say, revolutionary or anti-
Semitic or Fascist. The possibility must remain open at all times
that some group of people could only express their interest by way
of some such theory. Hence nothing may be excluded as such.

The appropriate image here is that of a blindfolded justice
(always a woman; a virgin?) holding the scales. Our pluralists
would install this figurine in front of the legislatures and executive
offices as well as outside the courts. Other political philosophers
wonder about how men are ever to learn what is just. Liberalism
has an elegant solution : let the just blindfold themselves. This self-
restraint is thought necessary because justice is meant to be guaranteed by the internal working of the system. It does not require
the aid of scheming ideologists. In fact, the case is stronger; the
one thing it cannot, in principle, tolerate is such scheming.

But does such a blind impartial mechanism exist? Is the
empirical presumption upon which this doctrine is based a fact?
The overwhelming weight of evidence now is that it is not. The
arguments adduced in Mancur Olson's *Logic of Collective Action*
are conclusive.[7] The actual operation of interest-group activity
serves best the interests of small, well-organized groups which can
compel all members to support their side. It works to the
disadvantage of large diffuse groups. It favours professional associations of doctors and discriminates against consumers, the unemployed and the elderly. In other words, the system favours those
who least need help. How does this come about? Olson's argument
is twofold: he argued, *a priori*, from the action of a 'rational self-

interested' individual to show that he will only support the activities of 'his' interest group under constraint where it is too large
for his own individual effort to make any appreciable difference;
and he argues from empirical evidence that doctors' groups –
which are in a position to require membership under pain of exclusion from professional office – are much better organized and
much more successful on behalf of their members' interests than
consumer groups. The latter, though in principle very large, can
only achieve any sizeable membership by offering extrinsic induce-
ments to membership such as savings on purchases from the local
merchants.

Olson's first argument begins by positing a 'rational self-
interested man'. 'Economic man' we might prefer. The chap who
decides – he always decides, never acts on impulse or fancy –
what to do by asking in each case 'What's in it for me?' In the
decision at issue, he has to decide whether or not to join 'his'
pressure group, say a union. Will he join? If the union is small,
affects only his works, and he would obviously gain by his joining,
he will. He will also join 'his' union where it is large and no general
effect can reasonably be expected from his joining *if* it either (*a*)
requires him to join as a condition of employment, or (*b*) offers to
save him large amounts of money (larger at least than his dues)
by allowing him to save a proportion of his purchases. Failing
either of these two kinds of extrinsic incentive, he will not join no
matter how effective the union is in securing benefits, such as large
pay rises, on his behalf. He will not join, lacking these incentives,
because he will enjoy the benefits of the larger pay secured by the
union merely because he has his particular job. When he considers
*his* joining the union, he realizes that there is nothing in it for him.
He would never join out of mere loyalty, or the romantic urge to
pull his weight alone, because that is not a rationally self-interested
thing to do.

One recalls that the notion of a rationally self-interested man is
but a refinement of the earliest Liberalism, though, to be sure, not
one which J. S. Mill liked at all, and one sees the trap Liberalism
is in. For it is the large groups of badly organized men, the unemployed, the immigrants, the uneducated, the poor, who most need
the protection of powerful interest groups – not the doctors. Since
these large unorganized groups are composed of people who, if
they were rational men in Liberal terms, would not join such

groups, the mechanism breaks down, and with it does the notion that Western government is government *for* the people.

This is not to say that Western governments are no worse than totalitarian ones, or that the rational man has nothing to choose between being, say, British or Russian. It is merely to say that Liberalism fails to establish, or at any rate add to, the case that he is better off British. Neither is it to say that pressure groups are not very important in Western politics, nor to deny that they are freer of government interference there than in the Soviet Union. But it is to say that the case for a blindfolded justice has not been proved. Justice would seem to be more than tolerance; or, putting the point another way, we may say that the tolerance supposedly characteristic of Western governments has not been tested. The operation of the system serves to prevent outside groups from making serious demands on the system. It is not as fair in its operation as Liberals would have us believe. Their theory is inadequate on the ground that they choose to urge its advantage.

### III

Conservatism, as we know it, arises in response to a specific historical phenomenon: Nazi and Soviet tyranny. Liberalism arises in response to that same experience. 'Totalitarianism' is the name commonly given to that experience. The name points to the fact that the ruling gang in such societies endeavour to spread their fiat throughout the country. The notion is that the distinction between private and public and that between official and unofficial cease to make sense. Everything and everybody is brought into the regime's ken. The Nazi practice of encouraging schoolchildren to report the chance remarks of their parents to the school officials is one powerful example cited by Hannah Arendt. The children are made to spy on their parents for the regime.

The intention of the Conservative and Liberal ideologists was to create a horrible image of non-Western rule and implant it firmly in the public memory. In each case, the image functions as a kind of 'Antichrist'. As such, it provides us with valuable clues as to the supposed nature of the Christ.

We have already seen that Conservatives draw a radical distinction between ideology-infested and traditional politics. Their

'Antichrist' follows abstract plans; their Christ acts on his intimations. Liberals use a similar device. They draw a distinction
between ideological (totalitarian) and tolerant (democratic)
politics. The two disagree about the nature of the 'Antichrist' and
the Christ; they agree, more or less, about who the 'Antichrist' is.

Perhaps the most important difference between the two anti-
totalitarianisms is that the Liberals have a much firmer grasp of
the nature and limits of contemporary politics. However one-
sided and rosy Aron's or Popper's view of interest-group conflict
is, there can be no doubt that such conflict is a very important
part of contemporary political action. Camus cites trade union
militancy as the epitome of intelligent moral political behaviour.
It is seen, by him, as activity within sensible limits on behalf of
large numbers of men. Without accepting that this is the case (are
Jimmy Hoffa and Les Cannon just two very different exceptions,
or definitive counter-examples?), no one can doubt that trade
union activity matters a great deal.

In trying to come to terms with it, and examining its moral
implications, Liberals are dealing with what is actually going
on.

Unhappy though they may be about some details, Liberals are
not in the politically ridiculous position of being against everything that has happened since the Renaissance. We may characterize the difference by saying that Conservatism knows only
what it is *against*; Liberalism knows, if only in schematic terms,
what it is *for*.

If Liberals are for a tolerant society, they are against an
intolerant society. Their quarrel with ideology is with its intolerance. This feature they see to be crucial. From the Liberal point
of view, ideology is intolerant political thinking. Aron praises
tolerance: 'If tolerance is born of doubt, let us teach everyone to
doubt all the models and utopias, to challenge all the prophets of
redemption and the heralds of catastrophe.'[8] Anglo-American
politics is free of such intolerance: 'The "American way of life" is
the negation of what the European intellectual means by the
word "ideology".' Our ideas, so far from being ideological, are
philosophy:

> By the same token, it must be said that the non-party state, the
> state of parties, in order to tolerate the pluralism of parties and

of doctrines is not devoid of doctrine, because the renunciation of violence is itself a philosophy.[9]

In the Soviet Union, on the other hand:

A single party, enjoying the monopoly of political activity, dominates the state and imposes its own ideology on all other organisations. Through the state, which acts as an intermediary, it has a monopoly of the means of coercion, and of the information and propaganda media . . . [this leads to] the use of terror.[10]

Crick agrees: 'We shall find there [in totalitarian countries] a direct attack on the idea of a diversity of semi-independent groups in society and an attack on the idea of the affirmative individual.' His contrast is with politics: 'ideological thinking is an explicit and direct challenge to political thinking'.[11] For similar reasons, John Plamenatz thinks ideologies lend themselves to this kind of thing.[12]

This assertion that ideology is intolerant political thinking leads Liberal thinkers to write of religion as a kind of ideology. For them the battle against ideology today is but an echo of the battle against religion yesterday. Thus they come to use the vocabulary of religious life to describe ideology. From this point of view, the association is to the common detriment.

Eric Hoffer's lively little book *The True Believer* epitomizes this aspect of Liberal anti-ideology.[13] Hoffer uses the vocabularies of both mob-psychology and Christianity to produce a picture of the motivations which lead men to join ideological movements and to describe the satisfactions gained from membership which is thoroughly distasteful. Hoffer discerns a strong connection between the lonely purposelessness of life for many; their willingness, nay, need, for a reassuring construction of social reality; their fervent, even blind belief in such a framework when an ideology offers it to them, and their complete intolerance of opposition to their ideology combined with a willingness to do anything for 'their' truth.

As a description of how people behave once in such movements and a theory about why they join in the first place, his ideas carry some conviction. Like Koestler, Hoffer is an ex-Communist. It is no disrespect to him to suggest that his theory is derived from an abstraction from his own experience. One might suggest that *The True Believer*, like *The God that Failed*, stinks all too freshly of godly conversion.[14]

From the Liberal point of view, the similarity of religious and ideological fervour and intolerance is too obvious to ignore. The inclination to see Catholicism (in particular) on the one hand and Marxism and Fascism on the other as twins, is reinforced by the accidents of history: Liberalism arose in the first place as a reaction against the former and now finds itself aligned against the latter.

It is also true that many of the features of the totalitarian ideologies (to use Liberal categories), especially Marxism, lend themselves to description in Christian, or at any rate religious, categories. The party are 'priests'; they share a 'faith'; the revolution is an 'apocalypse'; and so on. There are also similarities of action between the practices of the early Christians and that of the early Communists. Both groups were forced to organize in illicit cells. The members of the cells took the precaution of using pseudonyms in party circles to guard against police identification.

That there are similarities between ideologists and (at least early) religions can scarcely be denied. I am slightly uncomfortable about the implications drawn from this fact, however. For one thing, religious experience and language are such an important part of our culture as to be of little secular (if I may so speak here) interest. We could well speak of the split between classical and contemporary Liberalism as a 'schism'. Some of my colleagues speak of a 'lay' majority on the University Court. This does not mean that Liberalism is akin to Catholicism or that clergymen dominate the University. Too much can be made of the literal meanings of religious language.

More seriously, however, this exclusion of things religious and ideological carries the unfortunate connotation that anyone who takes his ideas seriously is in need of psychiatric help. In other words, the enthronement of tolerance to the exclusion of all other virtues requires an intolerance of anyone who takes his own ideas seriously. Robert Paul Wolff has made a similar point in *The Poverty of Liberalism*.[15] As he points out, tolerance of all religions is a possible stance only for the agnostic. We do not 'tolerate' people who think $2 + 2 = 5$; we teach them the truth. If, as a believer in religion, I believe that faith in my God will ensure

eternal bliss, and that ignorance of him ensures eternal damna-
tion, I have a duty to all men ruthlessly to destroy all other creeds.
I should begin by destroying Liberalism.

Extrapolating Wolff's point to political beliefs, one may fairly
accuse Liberalism of being at once singularly neglectful of its own
past and of its future. It is neglectful of the energy and courage
which was necessary to the establishment of each Liberal regime.
To put the matter somewhat dramatically, people actually died to
establish their independence from George III; others may have
to do so again to protect it from other tyrants in the future. A
theory which knows only the virtue of tolerance and compromise
is unlikely to inspire such men.

# Conclusion

The career of ideology begins, to all intents, with Marx and Engels's ideas about Hegelian social philosophy. We simply cannot say with any certainty why Marx used Destutt de Tracy's word 'ideology' to refer to these ideas. We do know that Marx's way of using the word is radically different from Destutt de Tracy's and that it has led to considerable subsequent confusion. Various writers have taken up parts of Marx's meaning and some writers have thoroughly muddled his complex, historically sensitive, term. These subsequent muddles have the effect of giving us a variety of meanings of 'ideology'.

I have shown in this book that there are at least three (this is not a magic number; it would suit my purpose just as well were there two or fifteen) importantly different senses of 'ideology'. To Marxists, 'ideology' is any theory which guides or acts effectively in the interests of the bourgeoisie. To Liberals, any theory is ideological if it teaches intolerance of other theories. To Conservatives, the hallmark of an ideology is an attempt to impose a rational systematic plan on society.

Patently, these notions differ from one another. My concern has been to show that these differences are neither arbitrary nor fanciful. Each social theory has a notion of ideology which suits its general outlook on political action. To be sure, if one could agree whole-heartedly with one or other of them, the problem would disappear; but this is not possible. Each has glaring detractions.

Putting the matter abstractly, we may say that 'ideology' is a pernicious form of thinking. The trouble with that formula is that it is so abstract that it tells us nothing – or almost nothing – about ideology. The question 'What is ideology?' is answered by begging it. That such a general formula begs the central practical issues can be verified by reference to what the various thinkers have in mind as an instance of an ideology.

In the post-Second World War intellectual world in which we live, ideology means different things to the different groups. To Conservatives and Liberals it means Hitler, Stalin, genocide, concentration camps, the bombing of innocent civilians (Guernica); generally it means totalitarian ideas. While Liberals and Conservatives may agree about that fact, they disagree about why such ideas are ideological and what ought to be done about it. Hannah Arendt wants something like a return to the principles of nineteenth-century Liberalism; Conservatives like Oakeshott are less easily satisfied. If I may, he is more radical; he wants a return to the misty comforts of twelfth-century England. When Marxists think about ideology, and about expunging it from society, they talk about moving forward (not back) to some different kind of society and political philosophy. Marxists have contemporary Anglo-Saxon political practices very much in mind when they think of ideology and its effects. To say that all this is somehow ideology, to abstract from the differences that separate these notions and try to dominate some essential ideology, is to miss what all the talk is about.

I do not deny that Liberalism, Conservatism and Marxism have common features. But that is another question. We may say, for instance, that each is more explicit about what it opposes than about what it is for. We may say, too, that each describes what it is opposed to as ideological. Again, we cannot but notice that deep in the heart of each theory is a central myth about society; each promulgates a myth and urges us to take heed. Liberalism and Conservatism promulgate a myth about totalitarianism; Marxism promulgates one about class struggle and revolution. These facts are interesting and important in themselves. Collectively, they constitute a large part of the political vocabulary of our times. Thus when a novelist like Koestler comes to write politically relevant fiction he turns to ideological myths. It seems to me, however, that our collective obsession with these nightmares is a great block in the path of an imaginative or creative political thinking. Further, it seems to me that precious little of the interesting political thinking of our post-war years has come from political philosophers (academically so defined) precisely because so much political philosophy is conducted in these nightmarish terms. But, tantalizing though such reflections may be, they are not our subject. How do we know that what Liberals, Conservatives and Marxists do is what ideology is? To end by taking this way out is again to beg the question. Perhaps these nightmarish features are characteristic of other thinking. In order to test that suspicion, one would have to do a thorough intellectual history of our time.

One thing, however, can be said: 'ideology' is a feature, even a key feature, of our political world. The fact is that we do disagree with each other about the central political and moral issues. We do not live in an age, like the Middle Ages of scholastic mythology, in which men fundamentally agree. *If* we did, there would be no problem about what ideology was because we should then have a common conceptual framework. But in that case, would we care?

In other words, if the world did not contain systematically pernicious ideas, would we bother to characterize them? I doubt it.

# Notes and References

## Chapter 1: The Idéologues

[1] A. L. C. Destutt de Tracy, 'Mémoire sur la faculté de penser', *Mémoires de l'Institut National des Sciences et des Arts pour l'an IV de la République: Sciences morales et politiques*, tome 1er, Paris, Thermidor an IV, p. 324.

[2] Ibid.

[3] *La Décade Philosophique, litteraire et politique par une société des Gens de lettres*, Paris, 30 nivose IX, p. 137.

[4] F. Picavet, *Les Idéologues: Essai sur l'Histoire des Idées et des Théories Scientifiques, Philosophiques, Religieuses, etc., en France depuis 1789* (Paris, 1891) pp. 624–7; also J. W. Stein, *The Mind and the Sword* (New York, 1961).

[5] C. H. Van Duzer, *Contributions of the Ideologues to French Revolutionary Thought* (Baltimore, 1935) p. 17.

[6] Ibid.

[7] L. Lévy-Bruhl, *History of Modern Philosophy in France* (London, 1899) p. 272.

[8] E. Condillac, *Essai sur l'Origine des Connaissances Humaines* (Paris, 1789) p. 124.

[9] Lévy-Bruhl, *History of Modern Philosophy in France*, p. 305.

[10] A. L. C. Destutt de Tracy, *A Treatise on Political Economy: to which is Prefixed a Supplement to a Preceding Work on the Understanding of Elements of Ideology* (Georgetown, 1817) p. 252.

[11] A. L. C. Destutt de Tracy, *Éléments d'Idéologie* (Paris, 1801) vol. I, p. xiii.

[12] Ibid., p. 4.

[13] P. J. G. Cabanis, 'Rapports du Physique et du Moral de l'Homme', in Van Duzer, *Contributions of the Ideologues*, p. 43.

[14] Destutt de Tracy, *A Treatise on Political Economy*, p. 7.

[15] Ibid., chap. 6.

[16] Ibid., p. 107.

[17] Ibid., p. 187.

[18] Ibid.

[19] Ibid., p. 254.

[20] J. Lakanal, *L'Ancien Moniteur: seule histoire authentique et inaltérée de la révolution française, depuis le réunion des États Généraux jusqu'au consulat*, vol. XXIII, 20 Mar 1895, p. 346.

[21] Ibid., p. 347.

[22] L. Napoléon, *Correspondance de Napoléon Ier*, no. 2306; cf. the account

in Lacour-Gayet, *Bonaparte, membre de l'Institut* (Paris, 1921): A. Guillois, *Le Salon de Mme Helvétius, Cabanis, et les Idéologues* (Paris, 1894) pp. 103, 121, 127, 156, 179–85.

### Chapter 2: Marx's Concept of Ideology as False Consciousness

[1] G. Lichtheim, *The Concept of Ideology and Other Essays* (New York, 1967) pp. 4–11; J. Plamenatz, *Ideology* (London, 1970) pp. 15–16. See, however, A. Naess, *Democracy, Ideology and Objectivity* (Oslo, 1956); R. H. Cox, 'On the Origins of Ideology: The Problem of Theory and Practice', *Papers of the Southern Political Science Association*, Atlanta (Nov 1970) p. 1.

[2] K. Marx, *The Holy Family* (London, 1957) p. 164, cited in Lichtheim, *The Concept of Ideology*, p. 6.

[3] L. Feuerbach, *Essence of Christianity* (London, 1854) pp. 20–1.

[4] See T. Bottomore (ed.), *Karl Marx: Early Writings* (London, 1953) p. 145.

[5] K. Marx, 'Contribution to the Critique of Hegel's Philosophy of Right', ibid., p. 43.

[6] Ibid., p. 44.

[7] Ibid.

[8] K. Marx and F. Engels, *The German Ideology* (Moscow, 1965) pp. 43 ff., 53, 61, 101, 183, 194, 254–5, 414, 461, 473, 490, 587.

[9] K. Marx, 'Theses on Feuerbach', ibid., p. 645 (originally published 1844).

[10] Marx, *The Holy Family*, p. 46.

[11] Ibid., p. 11.

[12] Marx, *The German Ideology*, p. 37.

[13] Ibid., p. 31.

[14] Ibid., p. 28.

[15] Ibid.

[16] 'Contribution to the Critique of Hegel's Philosophy of Right', in Bottomore, *Karl Marx: Early Writings*, p. 44.

[17] K. Mannheim, *Ideology and Utopia* (London, 1936) p. 37.

[18] Ibid., pp. 244 ff.

[19] Ibid., p. 23.

[20] Ibid.

[21] Ibid., pp. 77–8.

[22] Ibid., pp. 139–42.

### Chapter 3: Marx's Concept of Ideology as Apology

[1] See below, Chapter 9.

[2] K. Marx, *Theories of Surplus Value* (Moscow, 1954) part I, pp. 41, 68–9, 71, 77–9, 83, 85–6.

[3] From the afterforeword to *Capital* quoted ibid., p. 25.

[4] Ibid.

[5] Marx, *The Holy Family*, p. 176.

[6] Marx, *The German Ideology*, pp. 448–9

[7] Ibid., p. 454.

[8] K. Marx, *Capital: A Critique of Political Economy* (Moscow, 1954) vol. I, p. 620.

[9] Ibid., pp. 488, 648.

[10] Ibid.

[11] Ibid., pp. 61, 81, 82.

[12] Ibid., p. 760.

[13] See p. 26 above.

[14] Quoted in R. Meek, *Marx and Engels on Malthus* (London, 1953) p. 11.

[15] Ibid., pp. 17–18.

[16] Marx, 'Contribution to the Critique of Hegel's Philosophy of Right', in Bottomore, *Karl Marx: Early Writings*, p. 161.


### Chapter 4: Ideology within Sociology and Philosophy

[1] C. Geertz, 'Ideology as a Cultural System', in D. Apter, *Ideology and Discontent* (New York, 1964) p. 47.

[2] Ibid., p. 48.

[3] Mannheim, *Ideology and Utopia*. The immediate cause of his taking this position would seem to be his reaction against Lukács's *History and Class Consciousness*; see Lichtheim, *The Concept of Ideology*, p. 32.

[4] E. Shils, 'The Concept and Function of Ideology', in *International Encyclopedia of the Social Sciences* (New York, 1968) vol. VII, p. 74.

[5] Plamenatz, *Ideology*, pp. 137–42.

[6] T. Geiger, *On Social Order and Mass Society* (Chicago, 1969) p. 143 (posthumously published).

[7] G. Bergmann, 'Ideology', *Ethics*, LXI (1951) 205–18; P. Corbett, *Ideologies* (London, 1965).

[8] D. Emmet, *Rules, Roles and Relations* (New York, 1966); C. W. Taylor, 'Neutrality in Social Science', in P. Laslett and W. G. Runciman, *Philosophy, Politics and Society*, 3rd series (Oxford, 1967) pp. 25–7; A. MacIntyre, *Against the Self-Images of the Age* (London, 1971) chap. 22.

[9] D. Bell, *The End of Ideology: On the Exhaustion of Political Ideas in the Fifties* (New York, 1961) esp. 'An Epilogue', pp. 393–404; R. E. Lane, 'The Decline of Politics and Ideology in a Knowledgeable Society', *American Sociological Review*, XXXI, 5 (1966) 649–62, esp. p. 657.

[10] See N. Chomsky, 'The Responsibility of Intellectuals', in *American Power and the New Mandarins* (Harmondsworth, 1969) pp. 272–4.

[11] M. Williams, 'Up the Polls', *New Society*, 9 July 1970, pp. 61–2.

[12] R. E. Lane, *Political Ideology: Why the American Common Man Believes What He Does* (London, 1962).

[13] Ibid., p. 3.

[14] See T. Parsons, 'Authority, Legitimation and Political Action in *Structure and Process in Modern Society*, cited in D. Bell, 'Ideology and Soviet Politics', *Slavic Review* XXIV, 1 (Mar 1965) 596. See also C. J. Friedrich, 'Ideology in Politics: A Theoretical Comment', ibid., p. 612: '. . . it has become customary to refer to such action-oriented, programmatic congeries

of ideas as ideologies . . .'; and see A. Hacker, 'Sociology and Ideology', in N. J. Demerath and R. A. Peterson, *System, Change and Conflict* (London, 1967) pp. 481–98.

[15] Shils, 'The Concept and Function of Ideology', p. 74; and 'Ideology and Civility: On the Politics of the Intellectual', *Sewanee Review*, LXVI (1958) 450–80.

[16] Shils, 'The Concept and Function of Ideology', p. 68.

[17] R. K. Merton, *Social Theory and Social Structure* (London, 1957) p. 51 (emphasis added).

[18] Ibid.

[19] In part this would also require us to discover if they conceive of their interests as those of a person, a family, a class or a nation. It is not obvious that most people keep these things straight.

## Chapter 5: Milton's 'Areopagitica'

[1] E. Voeglin, *The New Science of Politics* (Chicago, 1952) chaps. 4–5.

[2] R. Hooker, *Ecclesiastical Polity* (London, 1907) vol. I, p. 153.

[3] T. Hobbes, *Behemoth*, in *Works*, ed. Molesworth (London, 1860) vol. VI, pp. 215 f.

[4] J. Gilles, *The Orations of Lysias and Isocrates* (London, 1778) pp. 476 f.; Isocrates, *Works* (London, 1928) vol. I, pp. ix ff.

[5] G. Kennedy, *The Art of Persuasion in Greece* (London, 1963); J. Milton, *Areopagitica* (Oxford, 1886) p. xxx, also p. xxxi for a different reason for citing Isocrates.

[6] J. Milton, *A Second Defence of the English People*, in W. E. Gilman, 'Milton's Rhetoric: Studies in his Defence of Liberty', *University of Missouri Studies*, XIV, 3 (July 1939) 11.

[7] Ibid., p. 13.

[8] Milton, *Areopagitica*, p. 2.

[9] Ibid.

[10] Ibid., p. 35.

[11] Ibid.

[12] Ibid., p. 37.

[13] Ibid., p. 50.

[14] Ibid.

[15] W. R. Parker, *Milton's Contemporary Reputation* (Columbus, Ohio, 1940) pp. 2, 25–6.

## Chapter 6: Paine's 'Common Sense'

[1] M. D. Conway, *The Life of Thomas Paine* (London, 1909) p. 26.

[2] T. Paine, *Common Sense*, in M. Conway (ed.), *The Writings of Thomas Paine*, vol I: *1774–1779* (London, 1909) p. 71.

[3] H. H. Clark 'Thomas Paine's Theories of Rhetoric', *Transactions of the Wisconsin Academy of Science, Arts and Letters*, XXVIII (1933) 309–35.

[4] Paine, *Common Sense*, p. 74.

[5] Ibid., p. 75.

[6] Ibid., p. 76.

[7] Ibid., p. 81.

[8] Ibid., p. 84.

[9] Ibid., p. 89.

[10] This information is extrapoled from the *British Museum Catalogue*. Several editions are undated.

[11] See also Shils, 'Ideology and Civility', pp. 450–80.

[12] R. Aron, *The Opium of the Intellectuals* (London, 1957) p. 112; see also M. Oakeshott, 'Scientific Politics', *Cambridge Journal*, x, 6 (Mar 1948) 351: 'Fascism *tout court* is, of course, something that exists only in the mind of the doctrinaire Communist; it is an idol of propaganda.'

[13] Williams, M. 'Up the Polls' *New Society* (9 July 1970) pp. 61–2.

[14] Conway, *Life of Thomas Paine*, pp. 23–4, 26, 29; A. O. Aldridge, *Man of Reason: The Life of Thomas Paine* (London, 1959) pp. 34–40.

[15] Paine, *Works*, vol. I, p. 395.

[16] Aristotle, *Rhetorica*, 1357b ff.

[17] E. Burke, 'Philosophical Inquiry into our Ideas of the Sublime and the Beautiful', in *Works* (London, 1890) vol. I. See Clark, 'Thomas Paine's Theories of Rhetoric', p. 316, where it is suggested that Paine read Burke.

[18] Burke, *Works*, vol I, p. 170.

[19] See M. Janowitz, 'Content Analysis and the Study of the "Symbolic Environment"', in A. A. Rogow (ed.), *Politics, Personality and Social Science in the Twentieth Century: Essays in Honor of Harold D. Lasswell* (Chicago, 1969).

### Chapter 7: Comte's 'Appeal to Conservatives'

[1] A. Comte, *Appeal to Conservatives* (London, 1889) p. 22.

[2] A. Comte, *A System of Positive Polity* (Paris, 1859) vol. III, p. 247.

[3] Ibid., pp. 8 ff.

[4] Ibid., p. 346.

[5] F. Manuel, *The Prophets of Paris* (Cambridge, Mass., 1962) pp. 263–74.

[6] J. S. Mill, *Comte and Positivism* (London, 1865) pp. 2–184.

[7] Manual, *Prophets of Paris*, pp. 158, 266.

[8] Comte, *Appeal to Conservatives*, p. 1.

[9] Ibid., p. 11.

[10] Manuel, *Prophets of Paris*, pp. 262–7, 274, 287–96.

[11] Comte, *Appeal to Conservatives*, p. 59.

[12] Comte, *A System of Positive Polity*, vol. II, pp. 346 f.

[13] Comte, *Appeal to Conservatives*, p. 93.

[14] Comte, *A System of Positive Polity*, vol. I, p. 253.

### Chapter 8: Koestler's 'Darkness at Noon'

[1] L. Goldmann, *The Hidden God: A Study of Tragic Vision in the Pensées of Pascal and the Tragedies of Racine* (London, 1964) pp. 278 ff.

[2] A. Koestler, *Darkness at Noon* (London, 1964; original ed. 1941) p. 226.

[3] Cf. M. Merleau-Ponty, *Humanism and Terror: An Essay on the Communist Problem*, trans. with notes by John O'Neill (Boston, 1969; original French ed. 1947) p. xxxvii.

[4] Ibid., p. 9.

[5] Koestler, *Darkness at Noon*, p. 224.

[6] I. Howe, *Politics and the Novel* (New York, 1957) pp. 19, 227–8.

[7] See G. Steiner, *The Death of Tragedy* (London, 1961) pp. 31–3, 232.

[8] Milton, *Samson Agonistes*, lines 80–2.

[9] G. Lukács, *The Historical Novel* (Harmondsworth, 1969; originally published 1937) pp. 150 ff.; Steiner, *The Death of Tragedy*, pp. 113, 195–7.

[10] See below, Chapters 10 and 11.

[11] C. J. Friedrich and Z. K. Brzezinski, *Totalitarian Dictatorship and Autocracy* (London, 1956).

[12] G. Lukács, *Solzhenitsyn* (London, 1969) p. 14.

## Chapter 9: Marxism

[1] H. Acton, *The Illusion of the Epoch* (London, 1955); Aron, *The Opium of the Intellectuals*; J.-P. Sartre, *Search for a Method* (London, 1963).

[2] A. MacIntyre, *Against the Self-Images of the Age* (London, 1971).

[3] A. MacIntyre, *Marxism and Christianity* (Harmondsworth, 1971).

[4] I. Illich, *Deschooling Society* (London, 1971) pp. 105–16.

[5] C. J. Freidrich, *Man and His Government: An Empirical Theory of Politics* (London, 1963) p. 90.

[6] See, for a different distinction, C. Arthur, 'Two Kinds of Marxism', *Radical Philosophy*, no. 1 (1972) pp. 25–8.

[7] G. Lichtheim, *Marxism: An Historical and Critical Study* (London, 1961) esp. part VI.

[8] See MacIntyre, *Against the Self-Images of the Age*, pp. 46–50.

[9] S. Avineri, *Karl Marx: The Social and Political Thought* (Cambridge 1970); D. McLellan, *Marx before Marxism* (London, 1970) and *The Young Hegelians and Karl Marx* (London, 1968).

[10] S. Ossowski, *Class Structure in the Social Consciousness* (London, 1963) part II.

[11] Lichtheim, *The Concept of Ideology*; D. Bell, 'Ideology and Soviet Politics', G. Lichtheim, 'Comments', C. J. Friedrich, 'Ideology in Politics: A Theoretical Comment', and D. Bell, 'Reply', *Slavic Review*, XXIV, 1 (Mar 1965) 591–621.

[12] E. H. Carr, *What Is History?* London,) 1962) pp. 132–3.

[13] V. I. Lenin, *What Is to Be Done?* (written in 1902) pp. 132–3.

[14] Ibid., p. 40.

[15] Bell, 'Reply' pp. 605–6.

[16] Lichtheim, *The Concept of Ideology*, p. 3.

[17] Ibid., p. 17.

[18] Ibid., p. 32.

[19] H. Barth, *Wahrheit und Ideologie* (Zürich, 1961).

[20] N. Harris, *Beliefs in Society: The Problem of Ideology* (London, 1961), pp. 2–6.

[21] Ibid., p. 267.

[22] Ibid., p. 2.

[23] Ibid., p. 6.

[24] Lenin, *What Is to Be Done*; A. Gramsci, *The Modern Prince and Other Writings* (New York, 1957).

[25] MacIntyre, *Against the Self-Images of the Age*, chap. 1.

## Chapter 10: Conservatism

[1] G. W. F. Hegel, *The Philosophy of Right* (Oxford, 1952) part III, 'Civil Society'.

[2] J. P. Mayer, *Political Thought: The European Tradition* (London, 1939) p. 192.

[3] See W. J. M. Mackenzie, *The Study of Political Science Today* (London, 1971) p. 14.

[4] M. Oakeshott, *Rationalism in Politics* (London, 1962) p. 169.

[5] Published together, ibid.

[6] B. Crick, 'The World of Michael Oakeshott: On the Lonely Nihilist', *Encounter*, XX, 6 (June 1963) p. 68.

[7] J. L. Talmon, *The Origins of Totalitarian Democracy* (London, 1952); C. J. Friedrich and Brzezinski, Z. K., *Totalitarian Dictatorship and Autocracy* (London, 1956).

[8] Ibid., pp. 80–1.

[9] See also G. Sartori, 'Politics, Ideology and Belief Systems', *American Political Science Review* (June 1969) p. 403.

[10] H. Arendt, *The Origins of Totalitarianism* (London, 1967).

[11] Ibid., p. 470.

[12] M. Cranston, *The New Left* (London, 1970); R. A. Dahl, *After the Revolution* (New Haven, 1971).

[13] See also R. Cox, *Ideology, Politics and Political Theory* (Belmont, California) 1969, pp. 367 ff.

[14] Oakeshott, *Rationalism in Politics*, p. 124.

[15] Ibid., p. 133.

[16] Ibid., p. 122.

[17] L. Polspisil, 'Legal Levels and the Multiplicity of Legal Systems in Human Societies', *Journal of Conflict Resolution*, XI, 1 (Mar 1967) pp. 11–12.

[18] M. Oakeshott, 'Masses in Representative Democracy', in A. Humbold, *Freedom and Serfdom* (Dordrecht, 1961) pp. 152–3.

## Chapter 11: Liberalism

[1] D. B. Truman, *The Governmental Process: Political Interests and Public Opinion* (New York, 1964).

[2] B. Bettelheim, *The Children of the Dream* (New York, 1969) chap. 18.

[3] K. Popper, *The Open Society and Its Enemies* (Princeton, 1963) vol. I, p. ix

[4] R. Aron, *Democracy and Totalitarianism* (London, 1965) p. 180.

[5] B. Crick, *In Defence of Politics* (Harmondsworth, 1964) pp. 34. 55, 111.

[6] W. Ebenstein, *Today's Isms: Communism, Fascism, Capitalism, Socialism* (Englewood Cliffs, N.J., 1967) p. 1.

[7] M. Olson, *The Logic of Collective Action: Public Goods and the Theory of Groups* (New York, 1968).

[8] Aron, *The Opium of the Intellectuals,* p. 324.

[9] Aron, *Democracy and Totalitarianism,* p. 236.

[10] Ibid., p. 185.

[11] Crick, *In Defence of Politics,* p. 34.

[12] Plamenatz, *Ideology,* p. 133.

[13] E. Hoffer, *The True Believer* (New York, 1951).

[14] A. Koestler, *The God that Failed* (London, 1949).

[15] R. P. Wolff, *The Poverty of Liberalism* (Boston, 1968) chap. 4.

# Bibliography

Acton, H. B., *The Illusion of the Epoch*; *Marxism–Leninism as a Philosophical Creed* (London, 1955).

Aldridge, A. O., *Man of Reason: The Life of Thomas Paine* (London, 1959).

Aiken, H., *The Age of Ideology*, 'The Nineteenth Century Political Philosophers' (New York, 1956); 'The Revolt Against Ideology', *Commentary* (xxxvii, 1964) pp. 29–39.

Almond, G., *The Appeals of Communism* (Princeton, 1964).

Apter, D., *Ideology and Discontent* (London, 1964).

Arendt, H., *The Origins of Totalitarianism* (London, 1958).

Aristotle, *Rhetorica*.

Aron, R., *Democracy and Totalitarianism* (London, 1965); *The Opium of the Intellectuals* (London, 1957).

Arthur, Chris, 'Two Kinds of Marxism', *Radical Philosophy*, No. 1, 1972, pp. 25–8.

Avineri, S., *Karl Marx: The Social and Political Thought* (Cambridge, 1970).

Barth, H., *Wahrheit und Ideologie* (Zurich, 1961).

Bell, D., *The End of Ideology: On the Exhaustion of Political Ideas in the Fifties* (New York, 1961); 'Ideology and Soviet Politics', *Slavic Review* (xxiv, No. 1, March 1965), pp. 591–621; *The Radical Right* (Garden City, 1963).

Benda, J., *The Great Betrayal* (London, 1928).

Bergmann, T., 'Ideology', *Ethics* (lxi, 1951) pp. 205–18.

Bettelheim, B., *The Children of the Dream* (New York, 1969).

Birnbaum, N., 'The Sociological Study of Ideology (1940–1960): A Trend Report and Bibliography', *Current Sociology* (ix, 1960).

Bottomore, T. (ed.), *Karl Marx: Early Writings* (London, 1953).

Brzezinski, Z. B., *Ideology and Power in Soviet Politics* (New York, 1962).

Burke, E., 'Philosophical Inquiry into our Ideas of the Sublime and Beautiful', *Works* (London, 1890), Vol. I.

Burke, K., *The Philosophy of Literary Form* (Louisiana, 1941); *A Rhetoric of Motives* (Berkeley and Los Angeles, 1969).

Burks, R. U., 'A Concept of Ideology for Historians', *Journal of the History of Ideas* (x, 1949).

Cabanis, 'Rapports du Physique et du Moral de L'Homme' in Van Duzer, C. H., op. cit.

Campbell, P. and Howard, P., *America Needs an Ideology* (London, 1957).

Camus, A., *The Rebel* (Harmondsworth, 1962).

Carr, E. H., *What Is History?* (London, 1962).

Cassinelli, C., 'Totalitarianism, Ideology and Propaganda', *Journal of Politics* (xxii, 1960) pp. 69–92.

Chapman, P. C., 'Stresses in Political Theory', *Ethics*, 1969, p. 38–49.

Chomsky, N., 'The Responsibility of the Intellectuals' in *American Power and the New Mandarins* (Harmondsworth, 1969).

Clark, H. H., 'Thomas Paine's Theories of Rhetoric', *Transactions of the Wisconsin Academy of Science, Arts and Letters* (xxviii, 1933).

Cohn, N., *The Pursuit of the Millennium* (New York), 1952).

Comte, A., *Appeal to Conservatives* (London, 1889); *Cours de Philosophie Positive* (Paris, 1830–40); *A General View of Positivism* (London, 1908); *A System of Positive Polity* (Paris, 1859).

Condillac, E., *Essai sur L'origine des Connaissances Humaines* (Paris, 1798).

Conway, M. D., *The Life of Thomas Paine* (London, 1909).

Corbett, P., *Ideologies* (London, 1965).

Cox, R. H., *Ideology, Politics and Political Theory* (Belmont, California, 1969). 'On the Origins of Ideology: The Problem of Theory and Practice' in *Papers of the Southern Political Science Association* (Atlanta, 1971).

Cranston, M., *The New Left: Six Critical Essays* (London, 1970).

Crick, B., *In Defence of Politics* (Harmondsworth, 1964); 'The World of Michael Oakeshott: On the Lonely Nihilist', *Encounter*, June 1963 (xx, No. 6), pp. 65–73.

Crossman, R. H. S. (ed.), *The God That Failed* (New York, 1964).

Dahl, R. A., *After the Revolution*.

Destutt de Tracy, A. L. C., *Elemens d'Ideology* (Paris, 1801); *A Treatise on Political Economy: to which is prefixed a supplement to a preceding work on the Understanding of Elements of Ideology* (Georgetown, 1817).

Drucker, H., 'Marx's Concept of Ideology', *Philosophy* (XLVII, 180, 1972), pp. 152–61.

Ebenstein, W., *Today's Isms: Communism, Fascism, Capitalism, Socialism* (Englewood Cliffs, 1967).

Emmet, D., *Rules, Roles and Relations* (New York, 1966).

Feuerbach, L., *Essence of Christianity* (London, 1854, originally 1841).

Friedrich, C. J., 'Ideology in Politics: A Theoretical Comment', *Slavic Review* (XXIV, No. 1, March 1965), pp. 612–16; *Man and His Government: An Empirical Theory of Politics* (London, 1963); *Totalitarianism* (New York, 1964).

Friedrich, C. J. and Brzezinski, Z. K., *Totalitarian Dictatorship and Autocracy* (London, 1956).

Geertz, T., 'Ideology as a Cultural System' in Apter, D., *Ideology and Discontent* (New York, 1964).

Geiger, T., *On Social Order and Mass Society* (Chicago, 1969).

Gellner, E., *Words and Things: A Critical Account of Linguistic Philosophy and a Study of Ideology* (London, 1959).

Germino, D., *Beyond Ideology: The Revival of Political Theory* (London, 1967).

Giles, J., *The Orations of Lysias and Isocrates* (London, 1778).

Goldmann, L., *The Hidden God: A Study of Tragic Vision in the Pensées of Pascal and the Tragedies of Racine* (London, 1964).

Gould, J., 'Ideology' in Gould, J. and Kolli, W. L., *A Dictionary of the Social Sciences* (London, 1964), pp. 315–17.

Gramsci, A., *The Modern Prince and Other Writings* (New York, 1957).

Guillosis, A., *Le Salon de Mme. Helvetius, Cabinais et les Idéologues* (Paris, 1894).

Gurian, W., 'Totalitarian Religions', *Review of Politics* (XIV, 1952), pp. 3 ff.

Hacker, A., 'Sociology and Ideology' in Demerath, N. J., and Peterson, R. A., *System, Change and Conflict* (London, 1967) pp. 481–98.

Halper, B., ' "Myth" and "Ideology" in Modern Usage', *History and Theory* (I, 1961) pp. 129–49.

Harris, N., *Beliefs in Society: The Problem of Ideology* (London, 1968).

Hegel, G. W. F., *The Philosophy of Right* (Oxford, 1952).

Hobbes, T., 'Behemoth' in *Works* (ed. Molesworth) (London, 1860) Vol. VI.

Hoffer, E., *The True Believer: Thoughts on the Nature of Mass Movements* (New York, 1951).

Hooker, R., *Ecclesiastical Polity* (London, 1907); Vol. I, originally 1594.

Howe, I., *Politics and the Novel* (New York, 1957).

Illich, I., *De-Schooling Society* (London, 1971).

Isocrates, *Works* (London, 1928) Vol. I.

Janowitz, M., 'Content Analysis and the Study of the "Symbolic Environment" ', Rogaw, A. A. (ed.), *Politics, Personality and Social Science in the Twentieth Century: Essays in Honour of Harold Lasswell* (Chicago, 1969).

Jansson, J., 'The Role of Political Ideologies in Politics', *International Relations* (I, 1959) pp. 529–42.

Kariel, H. S., *The Decline of American Pluralism* (Stamford, 1961); *Frontiers of Democratic Theory* (Vermont, 1970).

Kennedy, G., *The Art of Persuasion in Greece* (London, 1963).

Koestler, A., *Darkness At Noon* (London, 1964), originally 1941; 'Dialogue with Death' in *Spanish Testament* (London, 1937).

Kohn, H., *Political Ideologies of the Twentieth Century* (New York, 1949).

Lacour-Gayet, *Bonaparte, Membre de l'Institut* (Paris, 1921).

Lakanal, *L'Ancien Moniteur: seule historie authentique et inalterée de la révolution français, depuis le réunion des Etats Généraux jusqu'au Consulat,* Vol. XXIII, 20 March 1895.

Lane, R. E., 'The Decline of Politics and Ideology in a Knowledgeable Society', *American Sociological Review*, (31, 1966) pp. 649–62; *Political Ideology: Why the American Common Man Believes What He Does* (London, 1962).

La Palombara, J., 'Decline of Ideology: A Dissent and Interpretation', *American Political Science Review* (IX, 1966) pp. 5–18.

Lenin, V. I., *What Is To Be Done?* (Moscow, 1964).

Levy-Bruhl, L., *History of Modern Philosophy in France* (London, 1899).

Lichtheim, G., 'Comment', *Slavic Review* (XXIV, 1), March 1965, pp. 591–621; *The Concept of Ideology and Other Essays* (New York, 1967); *Marxism: An Historical and Critical Study* (London, 1961).

Lukács, G., *The Historical Novel* (Harmondsworth, 1969, originally 1937); *History and Class Consciousness* (London, 1968, originally 1923); *Solzhenitsyn* (London, 1969).

MacIntyre, A., *Against the Self-Images of the Age: Essays on Ideology and Philosophy* (London, 1971); *Marxism and Christianity* (Harmondsworth, 1971).

Mackenzie, W. J. M., *The Study of Political Science Today* (London, 1971).

McLellan, D., *Marx Before Marxism* (London, 1970); *The Young Hegelians and Karl Marx* (London, 1969).

Macrae, D., 'Class Relationships and Ideology', *Sociological Review* (VI, 1958), pp. 261–72.

Mannheim, K., *Ideology and Utopia* (London, 1960), originally 1929.

Manuel, F., *The Prophets of Paris* (Cambridge, Mass., 1962).

Marx, K., *Capital: A Critique of Political Economy* (Moscow, 1954), Vol. I (originally 1867); 'Contribution to the Critique of Hegel's Philosophy of Right' in Bottomore, T., op. cit. (originally 1842–3); *The Holy Family* (London, 1957, originally 1845); *Theories of Surplus Value* (Moscow, 1954, originally 1865); 'Theses on Feuerbach' in *German Ideology* (originally 1844).

Marx, K. and Engels, F., *German Ideology* (Moscow, 1965, originally 1845–6).

Mayer, J. P., *Political Thought: The European Tradition* (London, 1939).

Merleau-Ponty, M., *Humanism and Terror: An Essay on the Communist Problem* (translated with notes by John O'Neill), (Boston, 1969).

Merton, R. K., *Social Theory and Social Structure* (London, 1957).

Mill, J. S., *Comte and Positivism* (London, 1865).

Milton, J., *Areopagitica*; *Samson Agonistes*; 'A Second Defense of the English People' in Gilman, W. E., 'Milton's Rhetoric: Studies in his Defense of Liberty', *The University of Missouri Studies* (XIV, 3), July 1939.

H

Montefiore, A., 'Fact, Value and Ideology' in Williams, B., and Montefiore, *British Analytical Philosophy*.

Naess, A., *Democracy, Ideology and Objectivity* (Oslo, 1956).

Napoléon, L., *Correspondance de Napoléon* $I^{er}$

Oakeshott, M., 'Masses in Representative Democracy' in Hunold, A., *Freedom and Serfdom* (Dordrecht, 1961) pp. 151–70; Rationalism in Politics (London, 1962); 'Scientific Politics' in *Cambridge Journal* (x, 1948).

Ossowski, S., *Class Structure in the Social Consciousness* (London, 1963).

Paine, T., 'Common Sense' in Conway, M. (ed.), *The Writings of Thomas Paine*, Vol. I, 1774–1779 (London, 1909, originally 1776).

Parker, W. R., *Milton's Contemporary Reputation* (Ohio, 1940).

Parkin, F., *Class Inequality and Political Order* (London, 1972).

Parson, T., 'Authority, Legitimation and Political Action' in *Structure and Process in Modern Society* (Glencoe, 1960); *The Social System* (New York, 1964); 'An Approach to the Sociology of Knowledge', *Transactions*, 4th World Congress of Sociology.

Partridge, P., 'Politics, Philosophy and Ideology', *Political Studies* (IX, 1961), pp. 217–35.

Picanet, F., *Les Idéologues: Essai sur l'histoire des Idées et des Théories Scientifiques Philosophique, Religieuses, etc. en France depuis 1789* (Paris, 1891).

Plamenatz, J., *Ideology* (London, 1970).

Popper, K., *The Open Society and Its Enemies* (Princeton, 1963); *Conjectures and Refutations* (London, 1963).

Pospisil, L., 'Legal Levels and Multiplicity of Legal Systems In Human Societies', *Journal of Conflict Resolution* (XI, 1, 1967), pp. 2–26.

Printz, A. M., 'Background and Ulterior Motives of Marx's "Preface" of 1859', *Journal of History of Ideas* (XXX, 3, 1969).

Reis, R., 'Social Science and Ideology', *Social Research* (XXXI, 1965) pp. 234–43.

Rosenburg, M., 'Misanthropy and Political Ideology', *American Sociological Review* (XXI, 1956) pp. 690–5.

Roucek, J., 'The History of the Concept of Ideology', *Journal of the History of Ideas* (5, October 1944), pp. 480 ff.

Sartori, T., 'Politics, Ideology and Belief Systems', *American*

*Political Science Review* (LXIII, 2, June 1969), pp. 398–411.

Sartre, J.-P., *The Problem of Method* (London, 1963).

Seliger, M., 'The Concept of Ideology: The Case Against a Restrictive Definition', *Political Studies Conference* (U.K.), 1971.

Shils, E., 'The Concept and Function of Ideology' in *International Encyclopedia of the Social Sciences*, Vol. 7, p. 74 (New York, 1968); 'Ideology and Civility: On the Politics of the Intellectual', *Science Review* (66, 1958), pp. 450–80.

Shklar, J., *Political Theory and Ideology* (London, 1966).

Stein, J. W., *The Mind and the Sword* (New York, 1961).

Steiner, T., *The Death of Tragedy* (London, 1961).

Talmon, J. L., *The Origins of Totalitarian Democracy* (London, 1952).

Taylor, C. W., 'Neutrality in Political Science' in Laslett and Runciman, *Philosophy, Politics and Society* (Third Series). (Oxford, 1969) pp. 25–57.

Thompson, E. P., *The Making of the English Working Class* (Harmondsworth, 1968).

Truman, D., *The Governmental Process: Political Interests and Public Opinion* (New York, 1964).

Van Duzer, C. H., *Contributions of the Idéologues to French Revolutionary Thought* (Baltimore, 1935).

Watkins, F., *The Age of Ideology – Political Thought 1750 to the Present* (New Haven, 1964).

Williams, B., 'Democracy and Ideology, *The Political Quarterly* (XXXII, 1961) pp. 374–84.

Williams, M., 'Up the Polls', *New Society* (9 July 1970), pp. 61–22.

Wolff, R. P., Moore, B., and Marcuse, H., *A Critique of Pure Tolerance* (London, 1969).

Wolff, R. P., *The Poverty of Liberalism* (Boston, 1968).

Wolfinger, B., Wolfinger R., Previtt, K. and Rosenback, S., 'America's Radical Right: Politics and Ideology', in Apter, D., *Ideology and Discontent* (London, 1964) pp. 262–93.

Wolin, S., *Politics and Vision* (London, 1961).

Worsley, P., *The Trumpet Shall Sound: A Study of 'Cargo' Cults in Melanesia* (London, 1957).

Voegelin, E., *The New Science of Politics* (Chicago, 1962).

# Index